Publishing
Intellectual Capital

ISBN 0-13-021438-8

90000

9 780130 214386

Other books by James W. Cortada

EDP Costs and Charges

Managing DP Hardware

Strategic Data Processing

An Annotated Bibliography on the History of Data Processing

Historical Dictionary of Data Processing, 3 vols.

A Bibliographic Guide to the History of Computing, Computers, and the Information Processing Industry

Archives of Data Processing History

Before the Computer

The Computer in the United States

TQM for Sales and Marketing Management

The Quality Yearbook, annual

McGraw-Hill Encyclopedia of Quality Terms and Concepts

TQM for Information Systems Management

Information Technology as Business History

Second Bibliographic Guide to the History of Computing, Computers, and the Information Processing Industry

A Bibliographic Guide to the History of Computer Applications

QualiTrends; 7 Quality Secrets That Will Change Your Life

ASTD Training and Performance Yearbook, annual

Best Practices in Information Technology

Rise of the Knowledge Worker

Knowledge Management Yearbook, annual

Publishing Intellectual Capital

Getting Your Business into Print

James W. Cortada

Prentice Hall PTR
Upper Saddle River, NJ 07458
http://www.phptr.com

Library of Congress Cataloging-in-Publication Data

Cortada, James W.
   Publishing intellectual capital: getting your business
into print/ James W. Cortada.
   p. cm.
Includes bibliographical references and index.
ISBN 0-13-021438-8 (alk. paper)
1. Business literature--Publishing--United States. I. Title.
Z479 .C69 1999
070.5--dc21

                                                    98-51906
                                                        CIP

Editorial/production supervision: *Jane Bonnell*
Cover design director: *Jerry Votta*
Cover design: *Design Source*
Interior design: *Gail Cocker-Bogusz*
Page composition: *Scott Disanno and Daphne Victoria*
Manufacturing manager: *Alexis R. Heydt*
Acquisitions editor: *Jeffrey Pepper*
Editorial assistant: *Linda Ramagnano*
Marketing manager: *Dan Rush*

© 1999 by Prentice Hall PTR
Prentice-Hall, Inc.
Upper Saddle River, New Jersey 07458

Prentice Hall books are widely used by corporations and government agencies for training,
marketing, and resale.
The publisher offers discounts on this book when ordered in bulk quantities. For more
information, contact Corporate Sales Department, Phone: 800-382-3419; FAX: 201- 236-7141;
E-mail: corpsales@prenhall.com
Or write: Prentice Hall PTR, Corporate Sales Dept., One Lake Street, Upper Saddle River,
NJ 07458.

Printed in the United States of America
10 9 8 7 6 5 4 3 2 1

ISBN 0-13-021438-8

Prentice-Hall International (UK) Limited, *London*
Prentice-Hall of Australia Pty. Limited, *Sydney*
Prentice-Hall Canada Inc., *Toronto*
Prentice-Hall Hispanoamericana, S.A., *Mexico*
Prentice-Hall of India Private Limited, *New Delhi*
Prentice-Hall of Japan, Inc., *Tokyo*
Simon & Schuster Asia Pte. Ltd., *Singapore*
Editora Prentice-Hall do Brasil, Ltda., *Rio de Janeiro*

··

To my colleagues at IBM,
who taught me the business value
of sound thinking and clear writing

Contents

CHAPTER **3**

Types of Publications

41

CHAPTER **4**

How to Publish Articles: Some Rules of the Road

59

CHAPTER **5**

How to Publish Monographs and Books: Some Rules of the Road

81

Foreword

Knowledge management has emerged at the end of the 1990s as a strategic area of emphasis for organizations operating in highly competitive or changing environments. This decade began with many managers recognizing that core competencies presented a potential for competitive advantage. By its end, the question most asked was how to effectively build these capabilities and competencies through knowledge management. We have moved from an intellectual acceptance that what a firm knows (its individual members and the enterprise as whole) was important to a visceral sense of urgency in wanting to apply that insight to enhance economic performance. We went from defending the knowledge of people and institutions to the obvious recognition that this had always been essential to an organization's success. No less than Alfred Chandler, the great historian of American business, speaks of a company's ability to succeed as essentially rooted in its ability to acquire and apply learning.

For well over a decade, I have been working on the issues associated with the application of knowledge management in business environments. Through hundreds of projects, a dozen articles, and several books I have written, I have focused on the issue of how to go from the theoretical to the practical. Along the way, we have learned a few things about the application of knowledge management for practical advantage.

First, managers like to start implementing KM (the fashionable term now being used) by moving existing information around the enterprise more easily and in larger quantities. While KM experts may tend to question if this is true knowledge management, it does, at least, have the desired effect of creating the technical infrastructure needed later to make available databases maintained and supplied by competency teams. It is this introduction of such tools as Lotus Notes and expanded information search tools that, in particular, facilitate sharing of information in large organizations.

Second, there is a growing awareness among mangers that there are profound differences between information (essential messages) and more tacit knowledge (know what vs. know-how). Yet it is the tacit knowledge that is increasingly becoming the asset enterprises want most to exploit. Knowledge-sharing programs are cropping up all over the corporate landscape. Teams of like-minded practitioners are forming and working together as emergent competencies, teaching and sharing what they know. Expertise is becoming as valued in all lines of business as it always has been among consultants, professors, and other professionals. Management realized the wisdom in the old joke about the plumber who came into a home, did five minutes of work, and charged $75: $5 for turning a nut on a pipe, $70 for knowing how to do it.

Third, expertise within all sorts of organizations, whether in a commercial firm or in a governmental agency, has never been so valued as it is today. To a large extent we can attribute this to the significant shift of many industries to services where expertise does make a more apparent and visible difference. But we have also seen too much empirical evidence on the value of expertise—for example, in process management and improvement projects, management of complex projects, tactical experience in the creation and operation of call centers, and effective HR processes—to undervalue its worth in these areas.

It is this third area—one of expertise—that builds on the recognition by many corporations and agencies that training and skills development were crucial to their successes. This recognition came during the 1970s and 1980s, snowballed into formal intellectual capital programs in the 1980s and 1990s, and now positions many enterprises to lead with expertise in proactive ways. One of the first approaches involves disseminating knowledge that is already codified through the use of databases, newsletters, intra-personal networks, training programs, and so forth. A second concerns the use of publications. This has the dual advantage of allowing members of an organization to share codified knowledge with each other and with folks outside the enterprise, such as customers. And as James Cortada so clearly demonstrates in this book, the act of publishing forces practitioners to organize and improve their knowledge in ways that both makes them more effective personally and better able to share their insights with others. For these reasons, corporations increasingly are encouraging employees to publish.

From a marketing perspective, demonstrating the "right stuff" increasingly means showing customers better ways to use existing products or to apply the knowledge of a supplier more effectively. It is more than a truism that anybody can make a good product. We know from over a decade's worth of consumer surveys from around the world that the perceived and demonstrated quality of products has been rising steadily since the mid-1980s in most industries. For that reason, attaching new services to those products or traditional service offerings became crucial to a company's ability to compete and grow. Publishing in ways that help customers is a proven and economically attractive means of applying one's knowledge capital.

Cortada's is the first book that addresses the issue of publishing in a corporate environment, taking in the whole breadth of the mechanics of how that is done, linking these efforts to knowledge management strategies. As he often points out, any lone wolf in a firm can publish, but to energize those that have knowledge useful to the enterprise to publish in support of its business objectives, that is a very different issue. Cortada demonstrates how that focus is created both at the individual and firm level.

He rightfully begins with the individual because, in reality, the most useful knowledge in any organization is tacit and is embodied in employees. Motivate, focus, and support the publishing efforts of individuals and you are well on your way to using publishing as yet another tool for competitive performance. Cortada correctly points out that in most firms, publishing exists here or there, starts with an individual in one part of the enterprise or another, and eventually can be corralled into an effective performance-enhancing initiative. *Publishing Intellectual Capital* is both tactical and strategic, illustrates by example, but is ever-mindful of strategic intent.

Jim Cortada has over two decades of experience with publishing programs in commercial settings. He has mentored dozens of authors and helped public and private organizations launch publishing programs. The author of over two dozen books on management issues, he personally practices what he advocates. Cortada is also the co-editor of the *Knowledge Management Yearbook*, recently launched to organize what management is learning about the broad subject of KM. In short, he knows KM and has done what is in this book. It is an important contribution to the growing body of literature on how to effectively implement knowledge management strategies in both large and small firms today.

Larry Prusak
Executive Director
IBM Institute for Knowledge Management

Preface

This book is intended for those who work in the business world and want to publish articles or books, even possibly CDs and videos, but primarily written materials. There has been an enormous surge in interest in publishing articles and books by business people. This book is intended to help you understand what it takes to publish and how to go about it. It will not teach you how to write—you can go to a local university for courses on that—rather, this will show you how to take an idea, manage it as a project, and see the results sit on your bookshelf. Conversely, it will also illustrate how a corporation can encourage employees to publish within the context of a strategy to exploit intellectual capital. This is not a book about theory; it focuses on effective execution!

The need for this kind of a book has crept up on us very quietly during the 1990s. First, consultants and professors began to understand the value of companies becoming "learning organizations," which meant studying processes, customers, markets, etc., in an organized manner and then writing up the results of this work. Second, the concept of "intellectual capital" came into its own by mid-decade, as most companies began to recognize the economic value of their knowledge, core competencies, ways of doing business, and data about markets, customers, and products. Third, those in technical communities are increasingly participating in published debates involving their disciplines outside of their traditional circles of communications. In short, as we moved from a purely manufacturing climate to one characterized by services and compelling value, from technologies of all types being an expense to being strategic imperatives, communication through publications became imperative.

Running businesses has also become a far more intellectual exercise than ever before, as the body of knowledge about the field of business has grown explosively during the past generation. Monthly, thousands of articles and over a hundred books are published, just in English. Book publishing in the field of business is enjoying a Golden Age. Just in the United States in the 1990s, each year over 1,200 business books are published. Moreover, my own surveys of business publications during the early to mid-1990s clearly demonstrated that the best books are being published by business people; they are also outpublishing the professors! Some of the most widely read authors of the 1990s are not academics, they are business people and consultants. Nearly 100 percent of the quality literature, for example, comes from practitioners, over half the engineering and manufacturing publications come from practitioners or consultants, leaving to professors a monopoly on accounting and general management theory books. The best works on corporate cultural change, strategy, growth, information technology, best practices, manufacturing, supply chain management, to mention a mighty few, are coming from the business community. The same holds true in Western Europe, Latin America (especially from Brazil), and to a lesser extent across all of East Asia.

But publishing in a business environment is new to almost all participants. For one thing, most are just beginning to write and publish articles and books. Many of these new authors grew up in companies that discouraged publication; now they celebrate it! Why? Because publications represent "thought leadership" in an increasingly intellectualized business community. They also demonstrate experience and capability to provide services. These are important considerations given the fact that you cannot kick the tire on a service the way you can on a product which you can touch and feel. Intellectual capital and service delivery capability thus must be demonstrated differently—enter the article or book. That is why, for example, every major management consulting firm in the world now has an aggressive publishing program that would make many university business schools look like slow amateurs!

Yet, most corporations do not have a great deal of experience managing publishing campaigns, particularly long-term ones—a problem since the research-writing-publishing cycle can sometimes take years. But some best practices are emerging even in this area, and others can be borrowed from universities.

The heart of this book is showing you or your company how to get into print. It grows out of nearly twenty years of mentoring corporate would-be authors. I have learned that they ask the same kinds of questions and worry about the same issues, regardless of what company they are in. So, this book reflects their issues. In addition to the normal blocking-and-tackling concerns about defining topics, doing research, and getting things written and published, I will deal with a series of environmental circumstances different from those that exist in a university. For one thing, corporations normally do not give employees time to write articles and books the way universities do through summers off and sabbaticals. For another, intellectual capital is considered to be the property of the organization, whereas most universities consider it the professor's. Thus, copyright and competitive considerations are real-world issues filled with problems and traps for firms and authors. We will deal with them. In addition, I will cross to the other side of the desk and suggest how publishing can be encouraged by management. The final chapter is not the normal bibliography on publishing but rather a description of a process for learning more (with tools, e.g., bibliography).

The book is short and to the point—not an attempt at great scholarship—because I would rather have you invest only a couple of hours reading this and then say, "Got it, I now know what I have to do." Then, you can decide whether to publish and how.

You might ask why read my book as opposed to some else's. I have sat where you are, trying to write within a corporate environment—in my case, at IBM. But I also spent time in a university environment and have published within a scholarly setting. So I understand the differences between writing and publishing within higher education and in a corporation. I have published over three dozen books, some scholarly and others strictly trade or business management. I have also published over 60 articles in Europe, the United States, and in Latin America. My books have appeared in Asia, Latin America, Europe, and in the United States. I have learned the difference between a book published by Princeton University Press—one of the great academic presses of the world—and Prentice Hall, a major player in the business book world. I have published with both and with such other well-known firms as McGraw-Hill, Praeger, and Greenwood. There are differences in articles published in an academic "refereed" journal than in a slick business magazine. I have published in all those environments. I have written books in a month and others that took ten years; we need to discuss both extremes. As a member of various editorial boards of journals and as a manuscript reviewer for both trade and academic publishers, I have been exposed to the internal workings of a publisher, so I know how they decide whether or not to publish your opus! I am constantly writing book reviews of published material and have served on prize committees trying to recognize outstanding articles and books; I will share lessons learned.

This book is built on the shoulders of many writers in the corporate world, and not just on my own experiences. What made this book possible were the dozens of business people who had an idea to write an article or a book, the initiative to find out how to get the job done, then did it. They are the pioneers who recognized they had a contribution to make and that we were all entering a period when the ability to publish was increasingly becoming important. Mentoring article and book authors at IBM over the past twenty-odd years represents some of the best time I ever spent with colleagues. They were the ones who taught me what had to go into this book. I also want to recognize the support I have received over the years to encourage publishing within the firm by Michael Albrecht, Jr., the General Manager responsible for IBM's management consulting practices in North America. He recognized early on the strategic importance of publishing as part of our knowledge management initiatives and as a way of demonstrating thought leadership in the market.

I want to extend a special thanks to the team at Prentice Hall who worked hard to turn a manuscript into a book. In particular, Mary Lou Nohr turned noble intents into readable text, Jane Bonnell guided the book from manuscript to published volume, while Jeff Pepper showed faith in my work by agreeing to publish it. I was also deeply honored when Larry Prusak agreed to write a foreword.

Dear reader, I have one more observation to share with you. I know you will think you have no time to write articles or books. But you do. I wrote over 90 percent of this book on a laptop while flying in airplanes around the U.S.A. Look hard and you will find pockets of time sufficient to get the job done!

James W. Cortada

Publishing
Intellectual Capital

1

Why Publish?

Far and away the best prize that life offers
is the chance to work hard at work worth doing.

– Theodore Roosevelt, 1903

This chapter is about what publishers like to publish and why authors write. Publishing in the worlds of higher education and business are very different and so are contrasted. The chapter ends with a description of the personal characteristics of successful authors.

Publishing an article or a book is an important event in anyone's life, and for good reason. It is a monument to our efforts, proof positive that we can conceive of a topic in our heads, picture the book on our shelves, and then make that happen! For centuries, people who published generally have been highly respected, and sometimes locked in jail, but always noticed and taken seriously. But, having an idea for an article or a book and then going the whole distance, such that you wind up with a publication sitting on your bookshelf, requires a lot of work over a long period and investments of time and money by many people, not just by the author. Investments of time can be as little as several months for some light piece to over 40 years for the definitive book. It is not uncommon for book authors to spend two to five years on a book and then for their publisher to spend another year getting it published. These estimates of time are not for full-time work on a project, rather calendar time that passes since the

1

authors do other things simultaneously, like work. Articles can take weeks to write and sit around for over a year before they are published. But, the emotional and time commitment is enormous. So, all authors need to have really good reasons for going through all that work.

Perhaps nothing slows authors up so much, and in particular previously unpublished ones, as the fear that they will spend an enormous amount of time writing an article or a book only to find nobody will publish it. This is particularly a problem with people who write novels, collections of short stories, and poetry. It also happens to individuals who write nonfiction on subjects about which they are not yet recognized experts. And it always happens to people who write awful books! So, let's get the first fear of all potential authors—that nobody will publish your work—out of the way now. You already have reasons for thinking an article or a book is worthy of publication; otherwise, you would not have had the courage to spend all that time on it. But the big unknown from the author's point of view is always the one element over which he or she has the least amount of control—the publisher. So let's deal with that issue first!

WHAT IS PUBLISHABLE: THE PUBLISHER'S VIEW

Publishers vary widely on what they like to publish and the economic model by which they live, but both factors influence how they will react to a proposal for an article or a book. Some publishers specialize in fiction; others, only in business books; still others, in scholarly monographs. There are publishers who deal with everything, while others only do religious books or children's books, articles on specific industries or topics. Table 1.1 is a listing of specialties widely adopted by publishers.

The reason you want to understand publishers' areas of concentration is fairly straightforward. Publishers tend to publish articles or books in their areas of specialization more often than they publish on other topics. Once they have a specialty, they acquire the skills necessary to sell magazines and books on those topics. For

Table 1.1

Sample Listing of Book Categories		
Biography	Business	Biology
Current Issues	Management	Chemistry
Economics	Personnel	Computers
History	Self-Help	Engineering
Political Science	Technology	Physics
Technology	Travel	Sociology

example, the American Society for Quality (ASQ) Quality Press publishes many books on quality management practices, selling the books directly to the 150,000 members of the ASQ. Their members are not interested in books of poetry from Quality Press. The Harvard Business School Press and AMACOM publish business books that we have all come to expect are well written and on important business topics. With articles it is the same; the *Sloan Management Review* does not publish on tennis or cooking.

Publishers also operate on different economic models. Commercial publishers need to sell magazines and books that will generate a profit. University or think tank presses often would be happy just to break even on costs. How much cash a press generates depends on how many copies of a book or magazine they can sell. This is especially the case with books, so when publishers evaluate a proposal, one of the first questions they ask is: How many copies of this book can I sell? If the answer is more than the cost or profit targets required to make the project economically viable, then they go on to such other questions as: Is it well written? Is it on a topic of interest to the publisher or potential markets, etc.? Table 1.2 lists issues commonly addressed by publishers and can serve as a good list for you. The table grew out of the internal worksheets all publishers use to assess whether or not to publish books. These worksheets apply to articles as well, although usually only referees fill out such forms for an article. Often these internal proposals have to be filled out by acquisition editors on books that they want to publish. I find it a useful guide in determining whether the topic I have in mind would fit a particular publisher. It

Table 1.2

Sample Issues Publishers Consider in Their Cost Analysis
Length of book in bound pages
Number of illustrations
Trim size and number of columns
Permission costs
Author royalty terms and conditions
Required advance on royalties
Proposed print run (number to be printed initially)
Anticipated forecast of number that can be sold in year 1, year 2
Foreign language opportunities
Overall estimated production costs
Overall estimated marketing costs
Books in print or anticipated to be in print that will compete against this book

does not matter whether the publisher is a publisher of trade books (e.g., a biography of Madonna) or Princeton University Press publishing a text on religion in the Middle Ages. They all go through the same sorting questions to pick and choose what they want to publish.

So, what do they want to publish? All acquisition editors will answer the question in more or less the same way. They want good manuscripts on hot topics that can make them money. First, they want to publish articles and books on the topics in their area of responsibility. If an acquisition editor is responsible for acquiring and publishing on economic themes, that individual will want manuscripts on economics. Publications on other topics the acquisition editor will either ignore or pass on to the colleague down the hall who has responsibility for that subject. Most acquisition editors have to publish between 10 and 35 books each year; a journal editor may have to work with over 100 manuscripts just to get enough for a year's worth of issues. So, all editors are constantly looking for material.

Second, especially for books, editors look for material that their experience suggests will sell enough copies to make a profit for the firm. This is more than just simply a judgment call. There are some rules of thumb they follow. For example:

- Self-help books always do well if they are short and are published in inexpensive editions.
- Business trade books should be between 150 and 250 pages in length, with 200 to 250 about right, and sell for between $20 and $35.
- Business reference books can be longer and sell for up to $100.
- Technical books can be very long and can be sold for up to about $250 because technical people are used to paying those prices.

Magazine editors seek articles that fit the theme of their journal or magazine or the particular issue if the entire issue of a journal is being devoted to one topic.

Third, while editors are not always as current on a hot topic as they think, they do like to publish on what they think are current hot trends. Thus, for instance, in the early to mid-1990s they were publishing on reengineering and TQM. In 1995 and 1996 they deserted those topics and started rushing forward with projects concerning the evils of downsizing, the wonders of business growth strategies, and other books on change management, intellectual capital, and learning organizations (again, since learning had been hot around 1990-1991). In 1998-1999 it was knowledge management and the Internet.

There are three ways most editors learn about what to publish:

1. The experience of their press and other publishers with whom they have contact about what is or is not selling

2. Comments made by professors, consultants, and others that influence opinion, usually through private conversations and contacts made at national conferences and conventions (they attend all the big events, especially in the United States) or over the telephone

3. Their sense of what would work, given their authors and the quality of the books

Editors also are influenced by how they can market a book. A little-known secret is that they think in terms of where in a bookstore their product would sit. If you look on the back cover of most books published in the United States, you will see in the upper left-hand corner a topic suggested by the publisher. That hint is to indicate to a bookstore where on their shelves to place the book. If it says Management, for example, then the publisher intends for that book to be bought by business professionals. If it says Self-Help, it is intended for a different audience and, possibly, business professionals. As an author, you want to think about who should buy your book and where it will sit in the bookstore if it is a trade publication. If a book is to be sold by mail order, you, like your editor, must think of who this is going to appeal to because mailing lists have to be bought and flyers sent out to target audiences. Thus, a fat book on statistical process control techniques might go out to engineers in business, which dictates where advertising is done, whose mailing lists are used, and what the flyers say on them.

Magazine and journal editors have a slightly different problem. They have a defined readership that expects a certain type of material in each issue. Subscribers have paid in advance for a journal whose future articles are to be determined. Editors thus must be very sensitive to what their readership wants. Past issues of the journal are a good indicator of the kind of material that could be published in the future. Since the time it takes to write and publish an article is shorter than for a book, editors of magazines tend to respond to possible changes in the public's interest in a topic more quickly than does a book editor. Productive authors exploit that difference by publishing tentative, even controversial, material in journals first to see how they play before bringing out their book on the subject. Also, journals are a nice vehicle for announcing to the world that you are working on a topic—your turf—without saying so!

Publishers tend to specialize, and it becomes easy for you to find out what this specialty is. First, you can always ask an editor;

just call the publisher's office and ask for an acquisition editor in the field about which you are thinking. Second, they also know who does specialize in your subject if they don't. Third, you can look at who is publishing articles and books on your topic—something you have to do anyway since publishers will always ask you to tell them whose books are currently in competition with yours. Magazine editors don't ask that question because it is not relevant to their business.

The life of a book has become increasingly shorter over the last several years, so publishers will also look at how many copies can sell within a year; if a novel, often within three months. The days of publishers carrying books in inventory for many years are just about gone except for university presses. Academic presses still carry inventory for three or more years; trade publishers are in and out with a book in less than two years, as a normal rule of thumb. Then, they get rid of excess inventory; hence all those wonderful sales you and I get to enjoy at Barnes & Noble!

It is a given that a book has to be written competently, especially for a well-established and highly respected press. Publishers like Simon and Schuster, Prentice Hall, Free Press, and Harvard Business School Press want to preserve their reputation for quality. They frequently will get help in ensuring that they are making the right decision to publish a book by sending it out to experts to read while it is still in manuscript form, to determine the value and quality of the proposed book. This practice is also universal among all academic publishers in the United States and in most parts of Western Europe. Table 1.3 lists the kinds of questions a reviewer is asked to answer.

All publishers ask more or less the same questions. As a potential book writer, you want to keep these in mind as you craft your idea and write your book, even having experts read your material before approaching a publisher. I do that all the time—it is my sanity check that the project is worthwhile, and it allows me to fix problems before an editor has to say no to me.

Our emphasis so far has been on the book-writing end of this business because it is the most complicated. I will have more to say about articles in Chapters 3 and 4 because they also have characteristics unique to them, but we need to say more about books first.

Table 1.3

Questions Typically Asked of a Manuscript Reviewer
What is this book about?
What are its strengths and weaknesses?
How is it similar or different from other published books?
What are the author's qualifications to write this book?
What changes or improvements need to be made to improve the book?
Would you recommend publication? Why?
Can we use your comments for publicizing the book?
May we share your comments with the author?

In short, what is publishable? From a publisher's point of view, it is always a book that is competently written, is in a subject area familiar to the editor, and is one that the firm believes can sell enough copies to make a profit. Notice that we have not discussed issues that are relevant to authors: the message being delivered. Your book may have the answer to world hunger but will not be published if an editor cannot find a way to make a profit from it!

REASONS TO DO IT: THE AUTHOR'S VIEW

It is very important to know why you are writing an article or book, because such a project is time consuming and takes a lot of energy. Good reasons keep you going. Also, knowing why you want to write can help focus your research and outline of the material to increase the chances of meeting your objective. Since the biggest problem most authors face in business is the lack of big blocks of time to research and write, a strong commitment to the project is *the* key to getting the job done. So, taking the time to understand why your article or book is worth all the required effort remains essential.

While there are many reasons for writing, and often multiple reasons for writing a specific article or book, they can be boiled down to five. These are the ones we see within the business world all the time for nonfiction. Books of poetry, the Great American Novel, and short stories are different.

Because the publication will generate more business leads for me or my company. This is a popular reason for publishing either an article or a book, particularly within the consulting community. Surveys conducted by IBM and other companies of why customers buy consulting services clearly demonstrate that publications are the second most important reason why a customer would select a particular consulting firm (the first reason is references from friends and colleagues). "If you know enough to publish articles and books on a subject," the reasoning goes, "then you probably know enough to consult on that topic in my company." In other words, it is a third-party testimonial that you are an expert on a topic. That is why you will see many consultants publishing articles and books on the subject about which they teach and consult. Michael Porter publishes on competition and teaches and consults on the subject. Tom Peters publishes on corporate cultural innovation and customer service and lectures to sold-out meetings on the same subject. IBM consultants publish on the management of information tech-

"These days, it's publish or perish."

nology or knowledge management, then sell hundreds of millions of dollars of engagements on the same subjects. Michael Hammer publishes on process reengineering and then does process reengineering. In short, these examples provide a very good reason for business people to publish.

Publishing is also a relatively easy thing for business experts to do, since they would be writing on a topic they already know very well and about which they have a great deal of material, much of it already organized in logical groupings that can easily be converted into articles and chapters. And the audiences can be huge. An article in the *Wall Street Journal* could be read by nearly 2 million people; an article in *Quality Progress* or *Beyond Computing* by 150,000 professionals in that field of interest; books reach 1,000 to 400,000 people.

Because it will allow me to influence the debate on a particular issue. Sometimes ego is the hidden agenda, sometimes it is the fun of it, or even the source of thought leadership that naturally emerges from the mind of a knowledgeable person. Often, this base reason is what drives a business person with strong academic credentials. You typically see two types of people here: the first is the senior research or technical executive who has spent time both in teaching at a university and other years in the private sector; the second, the senior executive beginning to play on a national stage. An example of the first type is Lewis M. Branscomb, who ran U.S. government agencies, taught, was IBM's lead scientist, and wrote *Empowering Technology: Implementing a U.S. Strategy* (MIT Press, 1993). Clearly, he is trying to influence thinking on a topic, not trying to sell computers. An example of the second type is the memoirs of major executives, such as Lee Iacocca or, more recently, Bill Gates with his *The Road Ahead* (Viking, 1996), in which he engages us in a discussion about the future of computer technology and, more importantly, about the Internet. Senior executives are constantly publishing articles in major magazines in their industry as well.

Because I can make some extra money. While this is undeniably a reason, it is usually the least important and also the worst one because most people do not make a lot of money from books when compared to the many hundreds or thousands of hours they spend putting these together. You are rarely paid for an arti-

　　　　　　　　　　　　　　　　　　　Chapter I · Why Publish?

cle unless you are a professional writer. Either with articles or books, you can make more money spending the same amount of time flipping burgers at your neighborhood fast food restaurant. As it turns out, most business books sell less than 10,000 copies, with many selling less than 5,000. If you were to be paid the normal rate of about 10 percent of what the publisher sells a book for at wholesale, and with most books selling for between $20 and $30 retail, and 40 percent off at wholesale, you would see only a few thousand dollars coming in each year over the life of the book. There are some exceptions to the rule, of course. James Champy and Michael Hammer sold over a half million copies of their reengineering book, Thomas J. Watson, Jr., over 400,000 copies of his memoirs, and Tom Peters, nearly a million copies of his *Pursuit of Excellence* many years ago. During the 1990s, over 1,200 business books were published in the United States each year with less than a dozen per year qualifying as best sellers. The moral of the story: you better have a better reason; otherwise you should write a novel!

Because it is my job. On rare occasions, and most frequently within consulting organizations and research and development labs, employees may be asked to write an article or a book on company time, using the employer's resources. For example, there are organizations that conduct research and write up the results for a fee, e.g., a government agency. Think tanks are often asked to conduct studies about the environment, technological competitiveness of a nation, or other studies concerning national issues. So, that is work for hire. Other organizations, recognized as having a core skill, publish on a topic as an institutional part of their strategy. Manpower, Inc., for instance, routinely publishes the results of a survey it does several times a year about hiring practices of American corporations. Although the normal outlet for these kinds of studies are corporate newsletters or magazine articles, sometimes it is books, often written by a team of experts working within a company.

How does publishing affect knowledge management, often a growing part of a professional's job? One of the key tasks in knowledge management is the codification of what people and organizations know. The act of codification makes it possible to share insight with others in the firm and to expand the collective knowledge of the enterprise. To codify invariably requires that individuals write down information and insights in an organized, logical manner. That document is the vehicle for sharing knowledge. It is the same act as publishing. But more important, when you write down something in an organized manner, you improve your understanding of the topic, something we will have more to say about later in this book. The act of taking pieces of information and organizing them often leads to increased efficiency in work and, for the corporation, competitive advantages.

Because it is fun to do. I don't know if this is an ego trip (I think it partially is for me) or whether this falls into the same category as hobbies: playing golf or tennis, painting, refinishing furniture, or gardening. Is it a challenge, a mountain to climb, a way of demonstrating to your very bright older brother that you are smart? Like anything else, it helps to like writing, to have a curious mind, and to be able to organize large quantities of material if you are going to write an article or a book. It is an excellent reason that sometimes leads to other benefits, particularly if you become good at it. Your success is reflected in public recognition, royalties, and promotions within your company. Since most businesses only give lip service to encouraging employees to write, your motivation needs to come from a wellspring within you, unlike the case at a university where institutional support, encouragement, improved social status among colleagues, and rewards go to the professor who publishes.

How Publishing in Business Is Different than in Higher Education

The biggest difference between business and academic publishing is that in higher education it is often a major part of the job to conduct research and write, whereas in business it is not. At universities, professors are expected to do research and then to publish their findings. In fact, newly minted Ph.D.s (a research degree, by the way) normally have five years in which to publish a book if they want to remain as permanent members of a faculty (in other words, get tenure). And, they had better be publishing articles along the way to that book. Promotion to full professor at such a university requires yet another book and a handful of articles published in all the "right" academic journals. Scholarship is supported by grants that allow a professor semesters or whole years off from regular teaching and administrative duties to perform research. Professors have many outlets for their publications: university presses that will frequently publish on topics that everyone knows will not make any money and thousands of academic journals read by other professors in their subject area.

A professor's social standing within the academic world is helped and hurt by publications. Write a magnificent piece of scholarship, and your influence, prestige, and social position rise; publish a book that gets trashed by reviewers, and the reverse occurs. A productive scholar (that is, someone who regularly publishes good articles and books) will have the opportunity to play a leadership role within the university and in national academic associations. Even professors who teach at four-year colleges, where the emphasis is more on teaching excellence than on published scholarship, accrue prestige and positive rewards by publishing.

The situation could not be more different in the business world. For openers, businesses normally do not reward or value publication efforts the way they honor selling goods and services. They would rather have you spend an hour selling something than spend an hour writing. You will normally find that a company will not give you paid time off to write or support to cover research and travel expenses. Job descriptions and appraisal criteria speak about every other type of performance except publishing. If research is part of the job, in all probability your company does not want you to publish your findings for fear of giving away intellectual capital or helping the competition. In fact, if you do publish, even though you do not give away "trade secrets," you may be considered "different," an "oddball." People may question your commitment to the organization and to your career; thus, you run the risk of harming your future in the company. In short, the business world is not one that normally institutionalizes support for publication; it clearly does not have a supportive culture.

The one very big exception, and even then only partially so, is the consulting community. Its members outpublish professors year in and year out, for the reasons suggested earlier in this chapter. However, even here, publishing consultants often have to swim upstream. They are rarely given little or any time off from billable work to write, although they may be given time to do research as part of developing the firm's intellectual capital. They rarely are given any budget to handle the expenses of buying research materials, getting manuscripts typed and copied, postage, travel, etc., all normal expenses you will have if you write for publication. All consultants and business people, when asked why they do not publish, say the same thing: no rewards for the effort and not enough time to get the job done. Yet, there are enough who overcome these hurdles such that most trade business books today are published by consultants and practitioners.

The other big difference involves what gets published. I realize that, like everything else in this chapter, we are generalizing in order to highlight key issues. The same holds true for what gets published. Writers who work in the business community often publish articles or books that are practitioner guides to things, such as how to do something (e.g., running organizations, changing corporate cultures, managing a manufacturing environment, conducting appraisals, implementing ISO 9000). Academics rarely consider these kinds of materials as scholarship, but these clearly sell well and are popular with fellow business workers. User guides to specific pieces of software (e.g., the Dummy guides to computing) are written by experts on these topics and some become best sellers (e.g., guides to specific pieces of PC software, tax preparation guides).

Academics tend to publish books and articles that report on research and surveys conducted, with lessons learned. The case study approach is very popular, so too is presenting the basics of a topic (e.g., textbooks on management, accounting, marketing, and production control). Academics tend to publish through university presses, whereas business professionals usually work with commercial publishers. Professors are motivated to publish articles in scholarly journals; business people usually go to trade magazines. And for both types of writers, the opposite occurs often enough, too. For example, academics frequently publish business books with Free Press (a trade house), and practitioners often appear through Oxford University Press or the Harvard Business School Press.

There is a third community: journalists. It is not uncommon to see reporters whose "beat" is the business community, writing books about it. Almost all the books written in recent years about Bill Gates and Microsoft, IBM, General Motors, the changing telecommunications industry, and regulation and deregulation come from reporters. They also publish many articles on the same theme, usually short pieces that are either investigatory reportage or discussion of specific events. Too often, business people with inside knowledge of a particular industry feel constrained in writing similar articles and books while they are still active employees for fear of compromising their companies, while publishers suspect that there may not be enough objectivity involved in the effort.

Do You Have the "Right Stuff" to Publish?

So you have your reasons, you know what it is like to research, write, and publish in a business environment, but do you have what it takes to do the job? Most people who have never published an article or a book, or only one book, have a common nagging fear: "What if I do all this work and then nobody publishes my manuscript? What a horrible waste of my time!" I hope you never lose that fear because it will cause you to pick your topics well and work on them properly. But the fear is a legitimate one, particularly for a new author. Are there some key indicators of probable success in writing a manuscript and getting it published? In fact, there are.

1. You pay attention to the details of what it will take to write your article or book.
2. You are committed to doing the job by logging in the hours required, day by day, week in and week out, especially for books.

3. You like to do research, are constantly gathering material on your topic, and enjoy writing.
4. You are organized and tend to handle large volumes of data comfortably.
5. You have some experience either through graduate education or by publishing articles and teaching seminars.
6. You have worked in the field about which you are going to write for at least five years.
7. You get things done.

But the biggest indicator is commitment. You want to do this and will somehow find the time to learn how to do it and to chip away at it. This is not an activity that calls for inspiration, it calls for blocks of time of one to three hours once or twice a week for many years. Don't look for the opportunity to spend a summer on a Mediterranean island writing in the morning and hanging out at a cafe in the afternoon. That is *not* how articles or books are written. Learn from the humble bricklayer. This is really a project in which 1 percent inspiration is critical, probably 20 percent planning, 79 percent execution, and then another unpredicted 10 to 20 percent because nobody has ever figured out how to write their first article or book on schedule.

The Bricklayer

The humble little brick, so small, so versatile. With it we have built walls, homes, factories, cathedrals, and monuments. When laid in place, a brick can weather storms and time, serving us for centuries. And what about the bricklayer? What does this humble, often anonymous, worker teach us? For it is the bricklayer who gives bricks their purpose and power.

How he works is a lesson for us all because all great projects are like bricks and bricklayers, the composite of materials, ideas, and work brought together for a common purpose, a clearly anticipated result.

Cathedrals and great buildings made of brick are really the result of many bricks laid side by side or one upon the other. So many are needed to build a house, so many more to build a cathedral. Lay enough bricks together in some proper fashion and you have a home, a factory, or a church. Bricks are versatile; they can be used to make little sidewalks, short walls, water fountains, entrance gates, mail box stands, or they can serve as door stops and flower bed dividers.

Bricklayers understand the value of organized, purposeful work. A good bricklayer knows what he wants to build before laying brick. He carefully measures out the dimensions of the project, calculates the amount of brick and cement needed, and then invests the time it takes to lay them. Good bricklayers check their work row by row to make sure their bricks are straight and vertical. They periodically stand back and check if what the eye sees matches what the mind pictures. Ever notice the personality of bricklayers? They tend to be quiet, contemplative, even somber. They are creatures of routine, laying one brick at a time, one after another until either the day is done or all the bricks are laid. They will do this day after day, week after week, usually for the same amount of time, at the same time each day.

Quiet, methodical, yes, but what monument builders they are! The first skyscrapers were made with brick, the water tower in Chicago was built by bricklayers. You could also argue that the same skills were used to build the pyramids of Egypt as were used for Independence Hall in Philadelphia. Caesar called Rome a city of bricks. Bricklayers built the Smithsonian Institution's first headquarters, IBM's first factory, my first home. There isn't a country in the world that doesn't have brick buildings, sidewalks, monuments, and walls.

Bricks and bricklayers have long fascinated authors. A successful politician in eighteenth-century Virginia built a home out of brick, a university out of brick, and, fascinated with the possibilities of brick, the first serpentine wall in the New World. He was the author of the Declaration of Independence, the builder of Monticello, the founder of the University of Virginia—Thomas Jefferson, a founding father of the United States of America. Over a century later, another politician—this one in England—ousted out of political office at the end of World War I, bought a farm, wrote the first draft of a great work of English literature—*A History of the English Speaking People*—which he finished after serving in office during World War II, then wrote another masterful six volumes called *A History of World War II*. It is still the most definitive study on the subject a half century after its publication! During the interwar years he learned the skill of bricklaying and, as a hobby, laid bricks every day. He built retaining walls, sidewalks, stands, renovated parts of his home, laid a patio and, each day, also wrote his *History of the English Speaking People*, while meeting with politicians and national leaders to warn them of the dangers of Hitler's Germany. Winston Churchill was both a great author and a remarkable bricklayer working out back wearing his black suit and tie!

SUMMARY

For you, the business professional, getting published is tough to do. You are basically on your own and you might not have the right skills to begin with. That is the bad news. The good news is, people do it every day. I've talked with hundreds of writers over the past two decades, and they all say the same things:

- It took longer than expected.
- It was a lot of fun.

- ◆ They learned a great deal.
- ◆ They derived tremendous personal satisfaction.
- ◆ They would do it again.

In fact, many articles and books are written by previously published authors: sequels to earlier books, others on different topics, and still others outside of business, e.g., their first novel. Successful authors also share some common characteristics: they understand very clearly why they want to write and have a clear work plan for getting the job done. They do not hesitate to ask for help and to find out how others have proven to be successful.

2

Becoming an Expert:
The First Step to Publishing

Always believe the expert.

– Virgil, 19 B.C.

This chapter defines what makes an expert, why it is helpful to be one if you want to publish, and then describes how to become and remain one. It provides proven best practices and a road map for achieving expert status.

Most people think that it helps to know something about the topic they want to write about, and we also know that many people write about things they know little about. However, normally, authors of articles and books usually are knowledgeable about the subject matter. In other words, they have expertise in a topic; they are experts. So how do you know if you are an expert? How do you know when you know enough to write about your area of expertise? How do you become an expert? The last question is the most important because many people in business are experts but do not know that. So, we have to deal with that issue. In higher education, professors know that they know something about a topic because the culture of their world has built-in activities and signals that tell them they are experts. But those signals and signposts do not generally exist in business. You could be an outstanding expert on a subject and personally not know that, let alone have the confidence to apply your expertise to writing articles and books. Since it is universally accepted that being an expert is probably a pretty good way to start the process of writing and publishing, we should understand the subject. That is why the topic gets its own chapter early in this book. It also strikes at the essence of knowledge management in any organization—the tactic knowledge in people's heads.

W HO IS AN EXPERT IN THE BUSINESS WORLD?

An expert can be defined as one who has much training in and knowledge of a particular subject. Niels Bohr, father of modern theories of atomic energy, said that "an expert is a person who has made all the mistakes which can be made in a very narrow field." Expertise is the mastery of a body of knowledge and use of that knowledge in practical ways. Handling an axe well is a skill, not a subject suitable for expertise. Understanding how to manage a lumber company or analyzing how the paper industry operates are areas of expertise.

Over time, societies and companies have accepted certain general terms to describe topics or bodies of knowledge. These are typically reflected in examples like departments in a university, and the courses they offer. In business, these bodies of knowledge may be narrower in scope, e.g., the management of R&D in a high-tech arena. Fields have been carved out by people specializing in narrow bodies of knowledge in response to the demand for such expertise. For example, there are experts in how to manufacture certain types of computer chips, how to add preservatives to cheese, and how to perform certain types of surgery.

As our knowledge of things expands, the ability of an individual to know all things about a field diminishes. Knowledge in medicine, for example, doubles every several years. Consequently, new fields are created and recognized, emerging from a more generalized and broader earlier one. The knowledge of accounting broke down into ABC methods, auditing, and other subfields.

Information science broke down into programming, operations, systems design, and computer manufacturing. Computer manufacturing is broken even further into subfields of PCs, large mainframes, components of these machines, and then, of course, all the software needed to run these gizmos. The philosophers would tell us that no knowledge is obsolete. But since the definition of expertise in business also includes application of knowledge, that which is not applied becomes obsolete. In business, relevant knowledge leads to expertise and to experts, and to demand for their services, including their comments in articles, books, and presentations.

All fields of expertise are related to each other. Nothing ever happens in isolation from other activities. Expert fields are made up of a core body of knowledge, followed by building blocks of even more specialized or narrower fields. Accounting is a base field, ABC accounting a more specialized part of it. These in turn make it possible to develop skills. Over time, experts also redefine fields by broadening them to include ever-increasing amounts of related material from the periphery of their core expertise. Some experts acquire whole bodies of other known fields into their own. Thus, an expert on telephone centers might learn about telephone technology or customer service. An expert on statistics might also learn computer simulation. These are natural evolutions in the lives of experts, and they give deeper meaning to their work. Despite the tendency of individuals to learn more about narrower fields, experts eventually expand their definition of what constitutes the boundaries of their subject or start acquiring expertise in neighboring topics. These actions lead to the creation of new subfields because experts have a tendency to put new things together in different ways. For example, an historian coming into the business world might, after a time, begin to apply the lessons of history to current management problems in his or her company. It happens all the time.

Assuming that a field of knowledge exists, then learning a great deal about the subject can make you an expert. Knowing as much as there is to know about the subject and doing something with that knowledge can make you a great expert. Expertise is a prerequisite to responsible and important writing on a topic.

CHARACTERISTICS OF AN EXPERT

Is there a recognizable pattern of behavior that would lead you to believe someone is an expert? It is an important question because if you do not behave like an expert, people won't take you seriously and, if you are writing for publication, you may not get published. So although it may not be necessary to role play all the characteristics of an expert, it turns out that experts do naturally behave in a certain way. Since many experts in business do not know that they are experts and hence more than qualified to write on their subjects, it is important to recognize the signs.

Experts are people who know things in an acknowledged body of knowledge. Knowing more than anybody else about Wisconsin's gray squirrel will not do it. Knowing more about North American rodents might do it, and understanding the behavior of small mammals definitely does. Being intimately familiar with employ-ee suggestion processes in business, while useful, is not necessarily a recognized field of knowledge. However, understanding personnel practices and quality management, of which suggestion processes are part, is such a field.

Experts are people who are very familiar with a large number of facts about a subject and know where to get more facts in a timely fashion. Their familiarity extends to how that knowledge is applied and how to stay current on the subject. Experts, for example, read the major journals in their field and know where to find the important books, articles, or other experts in their subject area. They also access key Internet sites and pertinent databases. In short, they routinely use all the obvious sources of facts.

Experts know other experts in their field. This networking process is extraordinarily important and represents a major activity of any expert. Fellow experts can help guide you to additional information and insight in a field, allow you to test your ideas, and help you to define the boundaries of the field. They can also suggest topics for you to write about and then can critique your manuscripts to help improve them. For many experts, human interaction is the single most important way they have to gain new insights to stimulate their thinking and to sharpen their perspectives. E-mail, databases, and publications alone cannot do the job. Humans need to speak to other people to most energize their intellectual and practical growth. Experts are no exception.

Experts are people who display or practice their body of expertise. A doctor who does not practice medicine is soon not regarded as an expert in medicine, and you and I would not take our problems to that doctor. This problem is particularly critical in fields undergoing dramatic and rapid change, such as those that rely heavily on technology (e.g., computers, medicine, telecommunications). Displaying expertise is an elegant way of saying one practices his or her profession, with the difference that it may include teaching, writing, or commenting on a subject. Consultants, for example, do all three.

Experts are people who are recognized as such. This recognition results from several activities common to all experts. They apply their expertise; teach the subject; comment on it in speeches, on radio and TV appearances; do research to enhance their knowledge of the topic; and publish on the subject. They become certified as experts through such techniques as apprenticing as might a carpenter, earning advanced degrees as might an economist or computer scientist, or gaining professional certification by taking courses taught by the ASQ, DPMA, AMA, APCIS, or any other professional organization. Some companies also have pseudodegree or formal certification processes for similar reasons. For example, IBM's internal certification process for all key professions fits into this category.

Experts gain recognition by winning prizes and awards. Each well-organized subject area, industry, and company typically awards outstanding performance by members of its field. The military gives out medals and citations for skills displayed in combat. Businesses give awards to successful salespeople in recognition of both their skills and accomplishments in sales. Most professional societies have their own awards to recognize hard work, significant results, and demonstrated thought leadership (mainly as a result of publications). No IEEE Fellow, for instance, was ever an incompetent engineer or scientist!

Experts expand or change the scope and definition of a field of knowledge. This is a level of performance not reached early in the life cycle of an expert, but great experts all have this characteristic. This definition includes the scientist who provides a new way of looking at a subject, discovers new knowledge (e.g., DNA or life on Mars), or successfully applies new techniques (e.g., heart transplants or a new way to analyze a company's core competencies). When Dr. W. Edwards Deming began to apply statistical process control to business functions in the 1950s, he introduced new concepts to business management that today are parts of a body of knowledge called quality management, with its heavy emphasis both on rigorous analysis and a strong bias toward providing high customer satisfaction. These notions are now pillars of modern methods of management.

Sometimes, expanding knowledge is ignored for a long time. B. F. Skinner, a Harvard University psychologist, was ignored for more than 15 years by other psychologists while developing behavioral psychology. He even had to start his own journal so that he and his fellow behaviorists could publish their work! Today his work is widely recognized and accepted. Experts today find, for example, that their company is not interested in ABC accounting, or quality management practices, or teaming, and so the time is not yet right for your expertise. The problem is that experts are often denied personal recognition in new fields because the world is not necessarily eager to accept new knowledge. But generally, these experts, because they persist, gain recognition within their lifetimes.

Experts usually make a living applying their subject. We have long known that this task is all consuming. John Oliver Hobbes in 1902 put it well: "A man with a career can have no time to waste upon his wife and friends; he has to devote it wholly to his enemies!" More recently, economist Paul A. Samuelson said, "I have always been overpaid to do that which I would pay to do." And finally from that wise and clever expert on many things, Benjamin Franklin: "He that hath a trade hath an estate and he that hath a calling hath an office of profit and honor."

Experts have some commonly identifiable patterns of behavior that are widely recognized. They are in love with their subject and are constantly searching for more information. Collectors, for example, are experts; they are constantly hunting for new stamps, books, antique jars, old cars, political campaign buttons, or whatever else they collect. You see experts constantly hunting through bookstores for publications on their subject; willingly discussing their subject enthusiastically day or night and ad nauseam; constantly trying to apply their expertise to all that they do; willing to spend evenings, weekends, and vacation time on their topic. Their subject often consumes their time, energy, and enthusiasm. Hobbes is right.

They also exhibit intense intellectual curiosity about their subject and about how they and others deal with it. Experts become very introspective about their own relationship to the subject. They dig long and hard to understand both obvious and subtle features. When not dealing with their subject, individuals may seem dull and uneducated, but never when it comes to their area of expertise.

How to Get Started and How to Expand Your Expertise

The very first step in getting started is to decide if you already have expertise; my suspicion is that you do; otherwise, you would not have read this far in the book you are holding. Odds are that, at a minimum, you have the makings of an expert and, more likely, you already are one in a recognized field. Simply apply the definition of expertise and characteristics of an expert to yourself, and you will know for sure. It is important to acknowledge to yourself that you are an expert or on the way to becoming an expert so that you can have the confidence to continue, to improve, or to take advantage of your expertise. That recognition also helps you determine what you don't know and thus what you have to learn.

Second, ask those who know you what your strengths of knowledge are; they will quickly point out the obvious.

Third, what was your training? What have been your professional experiences? A Ph.D. in economics pretty much says you have some expertise in economics. Twenty years as an accountant in various accounting jobs delivers a similar message. Management experience in three different companies does the same.

You probably have some expertise today, whether you like the subject area or not. But it may not be so clear to you because you have not applied many of the conscious intellectual and practitioner habits to your skill. If you are a financial analyst but do not read the financial journals or new books on the subject or do not write or speak on the topic, you may think you are not an expert on finance. By the definition prescribed in this chapter, you would not be.

Getting started includes recognizing that you have a long journey ahead. Regardless of the strategy you employ, it will probably take you several years to arrive at a minimum level of significant knowledge about a subject area. It takes that long to go through all the basic material on the subject alone. Some topics take even longer, especially if they are topics with considerable current activity, such as medical knowledge. Knowledge management or corporate change management, as subfields of business, are seeing an explosion of literature at the rate of about 10 books a month and hundreds of articles annually. The American Civil War now has a bibliography of more than 20,000 books and is still growing. More than 150 magazines are devoted to microcomputing. Now add to this printed material, seminars, classes, conversations with other experts, TV programs, movies, and so forth, and you begin to see the size of the mountain to climb. But don't panic; although you have to keep up and read and understand things that have come before you, you do not have to read it all. Experts on the American Civil War have not read 20,000 books, perhaps just several thousand over the course of their entire lifetimes.

However, it is the nature of skill and knowledge building that they build on top of previous information, much like piling dirt on top of dirt to make a hill. It is no accident that graduate students jokingly refer to the Ph.D. as "piled higher and deeper." As a child you learned basic mathematical functions (addition, subtraction, multiplication, and division), then acquired additional knowledge (algebra, geometry, calculus, and statistics) that relied on these basic functions. The same notion applies to all fields. So, your first step is to identify what is basic to understanding a field of knowledge. Several practical steps help.

1. Go see a professor or known expert and ask for titles of the three or four books that are the modern basic introductions to the subject. Buy them, read them, and from time to time refer to them. They will provide basic information, as well as importantly defining the features of the subject, much like a blueprint for a house will map out living rooms, bedrooms, kitchens, and bathrooms.

2. Use these books to find titles of other publications that you should read next to broaden your knowledge. Also, go back to experts for their thoughts on additional titles.

3. Next, identify the key journals in your subject area and read them in two ways. Begin by reading the articles in current issues, looking at the themes discussed, advertisements, and conference announcements. Then, read the back issues for about five prior years so that you begin to understand the current issues in the field. You probably will find that your field has no more than three or four journals that are considered the comprehensive source of information (often called the "journals of record"). You may want to subscribe to these so that you don't have to go to the library every time you want to read them. Such journals, with their articles, book reviews, and advertisements, keep you more current on the topic than books can.

4. If your subject area has professional associations—and most do—join one or more. The benefits of membership are enormous:

   ◆ Access to journals and other publications
   ◆ Useful conferences and seminars
   ◆ Contacts with other experts
   ◆ Support in your search for information
   ◆ Companionship in your subject area
   ◆ Opportunities to test and apply your knowledge

- Recognition of your skills and knowledge
- Publication outlets

5. Attend at least one major conference in your field yearly, and more is better. Each subject area has annual megaconferences for an entire profession, plus regional conferences that meet in many cities annually and often monthly. These are excellent sources for information, for stimulating and informative discussions, and for networking with other experts. Plus, they can be a lot of fun.

6. Become active first in local, then in national and international associations. They all have committees that focus on various issues. By joining them, you learn, provide leadership, and get to influence the agenda of issues of importance or interest to you. You can begin this process almost immediately with benefit to you and the organization. Simply ask another expert in your field which ones are the best to join now.

7. Attend seminars and, if necessary, classes. Heavy reading of books and journals combined with attending seminars helps build expertise faster than by going back to graduate school. However, you may find it tough to practice medicine without a medical degree! Fortunately, most subject areas do not require that kind of certification, particularly new and emerging ones (e.g., expertise in object-oriented computing or process redesign). The benefit of academic course work is that you usually cover the subject in a broader, more organized manner, than in the seminar. However, you can take a shortcut to the bulk of the knowledge by using books, journals, and seminars. Furthermore, it is often difficult to find time to take classes if you are working.

8. Seek out opportunities to apply newly acquired knowledge. For consultants, this can be a simple process: they propose engagements that require them to apply the material. For an engineer, it could be applying new techniques

to daily work or conducting experiments on current projects. The application of newly acquired knowledge can take any number of forms such as:

- Providing content consulting and advice
- Teaching in the subject area
- Using skills to solve specific problems
- Testing knowledge against a client's realities or those of your management or department
- Applying the principles in the management of a business or department

9. One of the most useful techniques for keeping up, and one ignored by too many experts, is reliance on newsletters. There is hardly a subject area that does not have newsletters. Sometimes, these are produced by national organizations or sometimes by regional or issue-focused groups. These are useful for several types of information:

- Activities in the field, such as conferences and seminars, awards and other forms of recognition
- Recent, important books and articles in your field
- Major institutions and organizations in your subject area, with addresses and contacts
- Contacts, and fellow experts

Because newsletters are short, appear frequently, and are usually managed by competent experts, they represent the most cost effective and efficient way to keep up with your field. While there are thousands of newsletters and often hundreds in popular subject areas, it becomes quite obvious which ones are relevant to you. Some push a point, others represent entire fields. All are clearinghouses of useful information. If you had only $50 a year to invest in keeping up-to-date, newsletters are a better investment than books or journals. Most experts invest in a combination of all three.

10. Plugging into a company-sponsored competency is increasingly becoming an excellent tactic. Firms that truly compete on competency and are serious about leveraging knowledge both of an institutional (explicit) type and that of individual employees (tactic) invariably create centers of competence or excellence and a virtual fraternity of experts around specific subjects. They collect information, share insights, and do all the things experts do, except within the confines of the firm. All major consulting firms do this around the areas they consult on, product engineers share within and across divisions, and cross-functional teams routinely engage in dialog and projects that exploit skills that the firm has as a whole. Becoming a part of such a competency is more than a best practice: it is a legitimate way to use some of the time your employer expects you to work.

The suggestions made throughout this chapter can easily and effectively absorb your energies for the first three to five years. The key is constancy of purpose: keep at it every week, year in and year out. Odds are, you are already doing some of these ten suggestions. Eventually, you will look back and see a mountain of expertise that you have piled up rather painlessly. Along the way you will have learned a great deal about how to keep up with your field. Suddenly you will feel that you know the breadth of the subject, can put your arms around it, and are comfortable with its related ideas. You will know when that moment comes. When it does, you are an expert.

There is one more, all-important suggestion. Try early on to find a mentor with recognized expertise. Even if this person is only someone you go to on rare occasions, find him or her. Mentors help in several important ways.

1. They can help introduce you to your subject in a logical and organized way, much like teaching addition and subtraction before algebra.

2. They can teach you the values and attitudes of the subject and its associated professions, which ensures good work habits.

3. They can land you speaking engagements, get your early articles considered seriously by publishers, and project you into the work of key associations.

4. They can critique your writing to ensure what you produce is of good quality before you even attempt to publish.

5. They make wonderful, lifelong friends!

So, you think you are an expert, and you have been doing all these things. Good! Now, what's next? Becoming an expert involves learning what has already been documented, both by reading and doing. As already suggested, that is a three- to five-year process. The next phase involves keeping up. For this second period, doing, attending conferences, and reading journals, newsletters, and new books does the trick.

Also useful at this stage is teaching. If you can find opportunities to teach either in one-shot presentations, as day-long seminars as part of a project, or under the umbrella of a professional organization, do it. Teaching forces you to organize your knowledge logically. It lets you test ideas and facts with a live audience that challenges you, leading you to greater confidence in knowledge and opinions. Your audience helps you plug holes in your knowledge at a moment when you are most receptive to new information. Finally, teaching and lecturing is a wonderful way of establishing your credibility as an expert.

But how do you get to the third level of expertise—to the status of a great expert? Clearly, the activities cited above are basic and elementary, performed by all great experts on a routine basis. What great experts do is over and above all of this.

The requirements are few but important. First, you must expand the body of knowledge of the field and shape its issues. Second, you should do this sort of activity for a long period of time (10-20 years is normal). Third, great experts publish on their subject, in the most important journals and through the leading book publishers in their field. Fourth, great experts continue to do normal "expert" things well, while providing leadership within the discipline's organizations. Think of Peter F. Drucker as a role model, even though he is a professor. I aspire to play the same role, too.

Research and publishing are closely linked. Consultants, professionals, and professors have the opportunity to do a great deal of research, experimenting with new hypotheses and processes, testing assumptions, then drawing conclusions from their work. For consultants, for example, every engagement represents an opportunity to do research, to expand the limits of the envelope. Aggregating and publishing results of many similar activities or research projects improves the quality of the research and writing. Also, conducting widespread survey work that transcends specific engagements and incorporates use of others' research leads to significant expansion of knowledge and, hence, useful publications. Writing or speaking is relatively easy to do if you do it in your own field of expertise. Most experts do not realize how good they are at writing and speaking until they try it. Practice is required, of course, but building skills is facilitated by a clear understanding of the subject matter.

Experts publish in several ways. First, they write articles based on successful projects or research efforts; then, articles summarizing results of multiple projects. Next, they start on books that simply cover larger quantities of material and more complex themes. This is a multiyear strategy that works. If the quality of these publications is good and if they deal effectively with important topics, they earn you rapid recognition as an expert. As your experience and knowledge expand, you can move from reporting on subjects and events to broader reviews of existing bodies of knowledge or sharper focus on information. The great expert is someone who can command a large body of knowledge, report on widespread results of research (their own and that of others), and synthesize effectively with new insight.

As you move along the spectrum from novice to great expert, pressure mounts for every publication to focus on increasingly important themes, published in ever more widely read journals or through highly respected book publishers, and always with better-quality contents. After all, good and bad articles and books are published all the time. Write a bad book and it can haunt you for life; once it's in print, you cannot change it! (For the novice writer: yes, it is possible to publish a badly written book!)

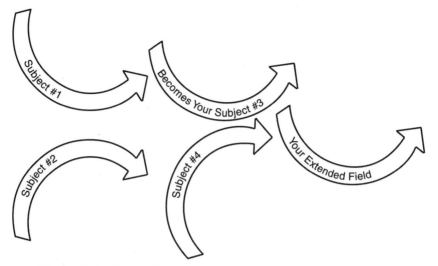

Figure 2.1   Time and Experience

After about ten years in their field, it is common for experts to expand their definition of what makes up a field. Perhaps out of boredom or curiosity, many experts begin picking up a new field as a novice, but the new subject is related to the old one. An expert in finance might also become interested in management. Someone specializing in the management of information technology and computers might also become interested in its history. Knowledge about manufacturing might lead to expertise in computing. And so it goes. Typically, this process occurs when there is some compelling reason to acquire a bit of knowledge in a related field and that initiative is expanded.

However, you still must keep current in your old field, meeting all the criteria for experts, while adding to your base knowledge in some new area. That is not impossible, and indeed, most seasoned experts do it. They ultimately blur the lines between two or more fields, finding it difficult to discern where one ends and the other begins. Figure 2.1 suggests the process of continuous renewal and expansion in people's knowledge and expertise that occurs if they are constantly adding to their expertise. When does the history of computing end and appreciation of patterns of information technology management begin? When is the subject of corporate tax law concluded and financial expertise begun?

It is this blurring of lines that sometimes leads to a new definition of a field. An obvious example is molecular physics: classic physics or biology? What about customer service: selling or marketing? What about quality management: management or statistical process control?

Leadership in national associations of your subject area is also important. Begin by joining associations, then serve on committees, next become president of committees, and, finally, assume leadership of the entire national organization. Often, the president and president-elect are chosen from the best of the published experts who have toiled in the vineyards of the subject for many years.

When in need of information, society's institutions, including your company, typically turn to major associations. Congressional committees routinely do this, as do news media. Once these organizations get your name, you will be called again and again as national issues or crises come and go. You will find yourself quoted in the national press. If you don't believe me, think about Tom Peters, Jack Trout, John C. Dvorak, and Edward Yourdon—all in business, not a single professor in the lot, and all became famous by writing on what they thought they were experts about!

You may be thinking, "Well, this is all well and good, but the time required!" The reality is, however, those who do, find the time. A greater barrier to carrying out the actions described in this chapter is a far more serious problem than time; you won't run into it in the beginning, but you will encounter it as you pursue expert status.

The problem is one of maintaining the necessary long-term focus. Very few employees in the private sector keep the same job for as long as it takes to become an expert. It is not uncommon, for example, to change job titles every two or three years. The American government says people now change careers on an average of three times in their adult lives. Most of us get new managers, along with their new agendas, every year or two. The point is, to become an expert you may have to add these expert-building activities on top of your various jobs, finding ways to weave your new skills into your ever-changing responsibilities. Professors do not face this problem because academics normally do the same kind of work, and in the same field, for their entire careers.

Corporations competing on competencies are not even aware of this problem, either. People are "hired" into competencies just like anybody else into any other business job. So they come and go, hence the rampant amateurism so often evident, particularly in American corporations. There are many exceptions, of course, particularly in product development and in R&D. However, the current emphasis on developing company-wide knowledge management infrastructures and the use of expert systems (including business intelligence tools) is an attempt to at least provide stability in corporate repositories of information. That is why, for instance, so often the first knowledge management initiative is the development of electronic file cabinets (databases) followed by the application of business intelligence techniques.

Authors and Bricklayers

Bricklayers and authors have much in common. They have much to teach each other about success, skills, and good work habits. For one thing, both are interested in results: the bricklayer, a building or a wall that did not exist before he began to work; the author, a published article or book on the shelf. For another thing, both have an idea—a vision, to use a popular term—of what the end result will be. They are very well organized: bricklayers and productive authors have a plan for their work, know what supplies (brick, cement, data, research, paper) they will need, and both master the use of their tools (trowel and PC). And they both value skill, expertise, and knowledge about what they do.

But they are more; both are artists. The bricklayer is interested in the beauty of his work, not simply in safety and functionality. Authors worry about the quality of their arguments and expression. Both are concerned about how their work—their monuments—will be received. There is the old joke about three bricklayers all working at the same site on the same project. A person comes up to the first and asks, "What are you doing?" and he says, "I am laying bricks." The person goes to the second bricklayer and asks, "What are you doing?" To which the bricklayer responds, "I am building a wall." Our questioner goes to the third, who is working side by side with the first two bricklayers, and asks, "What are you doing?" To which, the bricklayer responds, "I am building a cathedral."

Thomas Jefferson took forty years to build his home at Monticello; Winston Churchill twenty years to complete the brickwork at his farm. Both had to become experts on architecture and building materials, then they had to implement, to do, and then to do things of a great kind. Thomas Jefferson didn't want merely to write political tracts, he wrote the Declaration of Independence. Winston Churchill didn't want merely to write a book on English history, he wrote *the* history of the English-speaking world, and in six volumes! Both were honored in their time as great people, and both lived lives of great personal satisfaction. Some bricklayers build cathedrals, some authors write e-mail, others change how we think and act. The builder of walls and the builder of cathedrals share the same work habits, lay just as many bricks, and get paid just as much. Writers lay just as many bricks, too. You, too, can only write so many words a day. So, what do you want to do: lay bricks or build cathedrals? It's your choice.

SUMMARY

Expertise is the basis for knowing enough about something to write about it, the source of confidence to let you take that first step toward publication. Becoming an expert is no accident; there are specific things you must do to achieve expert status and to be recognized as knowledgeable. For different topics, expertise takes various amounts of time to achieve and maintain. So, how much time do you have to spend on it if you work in business? My estimate is that if you spent several hours per week in study and reading to acquire and maintain a skill, you should be in good shape. If you work in the area of the expertise, you still need this amount of time for study and reading. I can see you spending one to two weeks a year at seminars and conferences, and countless hours of professional association involvement. Writing and publishing are a different matter, and the subject of the rest of this book.

Before we move to that, however, let me emphasize once again that expertise is not an illusive objective; it is tangible and realizable by all of us. It is both tacit and explicit. Work and discipline are required, and there are some recognizable patterns of "best practices" behavior that we have come to expect of an expert. Increasingly in our information-focused society, our success depends on expertise. No longer a luxury or something to relegate to professors, expertise is up to you and me. Now, let's discuss publications, the probable reason you bought this book in the first place.

3

Types of Publications

A person who publishes a book willfully
appears before the populace with his pants down.

– Edna St. Vincent Millay

In this chapter, I define briefly different types of publications, when and why you choose one over the other, and
how they are deployed. My intent is to suggest that as a
writer or manager of a corporate publishing program, you
have options and that you, like most people, will use a variety of
these.

There are many types of publications and outlets for ideas.
They have different requirements for publication, are addressed
to a variety of audiences, and are normally prepared for differing
reasons. Why you choose one type over another, and then how
you write for it, are quite different than a professor might choose.
In business, we have different agendas that, in turn, lead us to different reasons for writing and for the format used. Often, successful writers in business will use more than one type of outlet to
deliver their message. Publications are a logical outlet of other
activities, such as marketing programs, documentation of best
practices, and development of tools for use by other employees.

Today, with the growing emphasis by businesses in displaying
thought leadership, options and outlets take on a seriousness not
evident before. The effect of publications on branding and strategy is driving this growing interest on where material should be

published. Increasingly, managers are engaging in the selection process, not leaving that to authors alone. Just as writers worry about where to publish, companies are beginning to concern themselves with the same issue, extending, in effect, their long-standing nervousness about what newspapers have to say about them. But, the discussion over these issues has to begin with an understanding of the various publishing outlets available to businesses and writers outside of academia.

ARTICLES AND WHITE PAPERS

Well, we think we know what articles are. Right? What about white papers? Aren't they the same? When is one more useful than another? Who reads these? Why? All good questions, all must be answered.

An article is, as you know, a short document published in a journal or magazine. Articles are normally shorter than book chapters and deal with very narrow topics. They are published in journals, magazines, or newspapers. If they go into a journal, it is directed at an audience of usually under 20,000 (except in the *Harvard Business Review* which usually is read by nearly 200,000 people). Such articles tend to be very formal, almost the length of a book chapter, and are usually dressed up with elegant arguments, lots of data, and footnotes. Often, methodology for findings is also described. Common examples of business or technical articles are presentations of major research findings, research techniques, or theories about how one phenomenon or another works. Journals are usually sponsored by universities, professional associations, or industry lobby groups.

Normally, one would publish in such journals to present a large body of data or to establish a professional reputation as a serious expert on the subject. This requirement for pseudo-academic credentials is particularly important for those involved in scientific and technical research who must develop a quasi-academic reputation so that they can interact effectively with other researchers and academics. Some journals also reach audiences that you want to speak to, such as senior executives with the *Harvard Business Review* or the *Sloan Management Review*. Normally, you decide to publish your paper by sending it out to several experts to critique for accuracy and intellectual (i.e., academic) quality; they vote up or down, and the editor takes their advice. This kind of journal is called a "refereed" publication because experts referee your paper. Table 3.1 lists a broad sampling of journals that publish technical and business articles. Some are refereed, and others allow their editors to select what to publish. All welcome articles by contributors.

Table 3.1

Sample List of Publications on Business Issues	
APICS—The Performance Advantage	Management Review
Business Horizons	Organizational Dynamics
California Management Review	Sales and Marketing Management
Executive Excellence	Sloan Management Review
Harvard Business Review	Strategy & Business
Inc. Magazine	Training
Journal of Business Strategy	Training and Development

Articles in magazines are normally much shorter, such as 10 to 15 manuscript pages, and often on much narrower topics. For example, instead of writing about a new methodology for reengineering (as you would for a journal), for a magazine you might write a short piece describing how you redesigned one process. Magazines publish articles intended both for very large audiences (e.g., *US News & World Report*) and others aimed at narrower groups (e.g., *TQM Review*). Typically, articles for these magazines are written in a more informal manner, usually without footnotes or formal academic dressing. The editor typically will make the decision on whether to publish your piece. Some editors commission all articles, that is, they are not looking for your contributions. Normally, the copyright page of the magazine tells you what the policy is regarding unsolicited manuscripts. If the statement is not clear, call the publisher and ask.

The reason for publishing in these kinds of outlets is that they reach much larger audiences or a greater percentage of a certain type of audience. For example, *Quality Progress* goes out to nearly 140,000 people interested in quality management practices; *Beyond Computing* is probably read by most Chief Information Officers (CIOs) in the United States. So, if you wanted to speak to quality experts or CIOs, you have two logical outlets for your message. Table 3.2 lists the various kinds of articles that normally are published by magazines. As you can see, there are all kinds of topics and ways to approach a subject.

Table 3.2

Sample Topics for Business Articles
Trends in types and uses of technology by technology, application, or industry
Case studies of specific projects that name the firm, hide the name, or are generalized
Summaries of patterns from several case studies or trends
Descriptions of specific business issues, with a point of view (e.g., ethics, quality is here to stay)
Background and report on a specific incident, history, or issue
Changes underway by function, industry
"How to" on any major business activity
Analysis of a problem or opportunity
Historical account of the role of an organization, person, company, or industry
Use of a tool or technique, with benefits and examples

So, when do you use one type over the other? Articles in journals tend to be preferred by writers of serious technical themes, whereas business management issues tend to turn up in trade magazines. Some people publish in both kinds of publications. For example, you could write a long piece on how to develop balanced performance measurements for manufacturing operations, but for a magazine you could also develop a short article describing how those measurements are applied in your factory.

What about articles in newspapers and newsletters? These are always very short—typically less than 1,000 words in length—and concentrate on two types of issues: news of an event, or an opinion about a topic. Newsletters might contain an article you wrote about what your organization is doing, whereas in a newspaper it might be your opinion about a business issue or trend. Newspapers will publish articles by business employees who are not journalists but who are acknowledged experts on a subject or who write very well. *The Wall Street Journal*, for example, carries guest articles of opinion; *The Chronicle of Higher Education* devotes its back page to the same thing.

When writing a book, you will accumulate a great deal of material that you want to use but that just doesn't fit in the book because it is out of scope. So, what do you do with it? Write it up as articles for journals and magazines. That way, you don't let your book wander all over the place; it remains tightly on the path you set out for it in the first place. Just about every book author in business has leftovers; these are perfect for articles.

Book authors have other reasons for writing articles. Long before you publish a book, it is useful to have a reputation as being an expert on the book's topic—it makes it easier to sell the book to a publisher. Publishing articles before your book comes out is a good way to market yourself and your company. It can also help a book. Notice how just about every book author published by the Harvard Business School Press or Free Press just happens to publish an article on the same topic in the same month as the volume appears in print? That is no accident; it helps sell books! Some authors also use articles as a way of staking out their territory to scare off competition. For example, in the late 1980s, I did research for a history of the origins of the computer industry and knew it would take me (or anybody else attempting to do the same) years to do the job. To scare off would-be rivals, I wrote articles and gave presentations on the topic. By doing so I was signaling that "Hey, I am way through the research and on to writing, so stay away." It worked! While two books on the same subject are O.K., the second person trying to get into print would have a harder time convincing a publisher to invest in his or her book.

Where do white papers fit in? White papers are like articles except they are not published in journals or magazines. They may, in some revised form, eventually be published in journals or magazines. White papers are privately printed (by you or some organization for very limited distribution) or simply cranked out on the oversized copier in your company's mail-room. There are various reasons for writing white papers. It is a convenient vehicle for putting your ideas down on paper to share with knowledgeable people who can help you refine your thinking and expression, like an early draft of an article. You can use a white paper to circulate your ideas among a limited number of people whom you want to influence. For example, a consultant who is an expert on the logistics of using the Internet, and consults on the topic, might logically produce such a paper to be read by potential clients. White papers are often published by service organizations (e.g., consultants and industry associations) to define topics, take a stand on issues, influence groups, and to establish personal credibility as experts. Publishing is hassle free, cheap, and quick. You also control who typically gets a copy of the paper. I like white papers for launching debates on critical issues within my company and as a way of getting hot information out fast to our customers.

White papers can be short or long and can look like a college term paper or have the appearance of a slick reprint of an article on glossy paper and in four colors. Why you wrote the paper determines whether it goes out the door in blue jeans or dressed for a formal dance. Normally, these papers are published with the blessings of your company and thus are an adjunct to whatever work you are doing. They most often are yet another communications vehicle aimed at colleagues or customers. Companies use these as effective marketing messages, some anonymous, others with the name of the authors. White papers are very popular with industrial researchers in laboratories and product development departments, management consultants, and senior executives (and would-be executives!).

It is not uncommon for someone in business to first write one or more white papers on a topic, then turn these or other manuscripts into articles, and finally expand them into book-length publications. Academics do this all the time, but with a slight twist. They typically will begin with a presentation at a conference, which they read so they have a text, then move to publication of a refined version of the presentation as an article, and finally they turn the stuff into a chapter in a book. Business professionals also make presentations, although they typically do not read a paper; instead, they talk about the topic from an outline. They might next produce a white paper as a handout, then move either to articles or a book.

So, articles and white papers have their place and are written as part of an outward-reach strategy tied to what an author does for a living or what a company sells and services. And that makes sense because these papers are normally written by people about what they do and thus are prescriptive in nature (e.g., on how or what, why to do, often with case studies). They can be very quick and easy to write because they are short and about something the writer is an expert on. The best book writers begin with white papers, move to articles, and finally to a book. That is how this book on publishing intellectual capital came together as a set of ideas. Running seminars around its issues firmed them up, ensured I was on target, and that the explanations at least made sense to the target audience for which this book is intended.

Monographs and Books

Monographs. Aren't they those narrow books professors write on some obscure topic, like Romanticism in Nineteenth-Century French Literature? Yes, in academic circles these are books based on large bodies of research on narrow topics, often published by university presses and intended for other scholars to read. I once heard a professor define a scholarly monograph as a publication that only six other people in the world would either appreciate or read! But in the business world, the term monograph has a slightly different meaning. Normally, a monograph in business has some or all of the following characteristics:

- It is longer than a journal article but shorter than a book (e.g., 25-125 pages in length).

- It is published by a company or an industry/professional association (e.g., by IBM Global Services, LOMA, APICS, or the Conference Board).

- It is on a narrow topic and will have only several chapters (e.g., on managing software programming projects, implementing ABC accounting techniques).

- It is intended for an audience that needs a level of detail beyond an article but less than a book.

Monographs are very popular with consulting firms because they serve as a vehicle for demonstrating thought leadership and expertise—two critical conditions that must be met in order to close business. Engineers and scientists working in business tend to publish articles more but will often produce monographs for use by colleagues in the same company (e.g., like user manuals). Business monographs have very limited circulation because they normally are not available to the general public. Although they may be for sale, often it is at a very high price, for example, $300 to $10,000 for a research report, whereas a book might only cost $25! They are, after all, intended for a very restricted audience. Some consulting monographs, for example, are restricted to members of the firm or to their clients; thus, if you worked for a competitor, you would not readily be able to get your hands on one of these. Most management consulting firms publish monographs and by policy or practice restrict circulation of these documents.

Let's talk about consultants for a moment. A very popular service consultants perform is to conduct a study for a group of clients who pay to participate in the work and then receive exclusively the final report. Clients want the material kept restricted to themselves because it could provide them with a competitive advantage over rivals. This report is often published as a monograph by the consulting firm providing the service. Many benchmark studies currently being conducted fall into this category. So, too, are specialized studies commissioned on such topics as specific market opportunities, descriptions of key competitors, and technical issues related to proposed products or government regulatory practices.

Most business monographs are not written part-time by employees who want to rush into print. They typically are part of one's job, done on company time, and for which one is judged at appraisal time. Authors of such publications often will publish articles that summarize the contents of such monographs, a good example of reusing material in more than one format.

Then there are books, publications that are produced by a publisher, sold to the public, and for which the author (or his company) receives royalties. There are many types of books; Table 3.3 lists the different kinds normally coming out of the business world. Notice that not all books are written, that is, not all are narratives. Some are collections of papers or facts. Table 3.4 lists the obvious reasons or purposes for writing each type. So, just as with articles, you have to decide why you want to write a book and for whom it is intended.

Table 3.3

Types of Books Published on Business
Textbooks on key functions (e.g., accounting, marketing, management, and engineering)
Case studies of innovation
Company histories
Biographies and memoirs of major business figures
Descriptions, analyses, and histories of industries, technologies, and products
Economic analyses of industries, national economies
"How to" books on applying methodologies (e.g., process improvement), techniques, and strategies (e.g., mass customization)
Descriptions on the use of technologies (e.g., marketing on the Internet)
Nature of specific technologies and their consequences on society and business
Quality management
Knowledge management
Descriptions of specific processes or functions (e.g., recruiting, human resources)
Training materials

Table 3.4

Why Books Are Written	
Type of Book	Reason for Writing
Descriptions of functions and processes	To establish credibility on how to do these
Analyses of industries, technologies, and economies	To establish credibility; to report on R&D
Strategic proposals, such as the use of reengineering	To generate business leads
Textbooks and training materials	To teach and sell training courses
Case studies and survey results	To establish institutional branding and to gain recognition
Tool descriptions	To communicate how to use the tools and to sell products and services

Books tend to be longer than monographs, but increasingly, audiences for business books want short ones. Michael Porter can write a 500-page book, and we will all go out and buy it. But someone who is not known or who is writing on a narrow topic had better be writing a shorter book if he or she expects to have it published, let alone read. A good rule of thumb is to write a business book that is somewhere between 200 and 300 pages long. That size allows you to cover just about any topic with reasonable space. I know, at the same time you can point to 400-page books that do the same thing, but the 200-300 page advice is simply a guideline. A 200- to 300-page book might have 7 to 8 chapters or up to 14 to 18 chapters. Just as people today prefer shorter books, they also like shorter chapters (e.g., 15-20 pages instead of the more traditional 25-50 page variety). In the end, you have to decide. But the point is, bigger is not necessarily better! Better would be two 200- to 300-page books instead of one 400-page tome.

Books are written for the same reasons as articles: to establish credibility, to bring new knowledge to market, and to advertise one's expertise. But because books take more time to write than articles, they require greater personal and institutional commitment. They take up many weekends and, if done on company time, many months. So, you really have to want to write a book to do it. While I will later discuss this commitment, let me point out here that books are very effective in meeting the objectives for writing them. In a study I did for IBM on how clients choose consultants, I found that after references and ideas from friends, books and articles represent the second most important vehicle by which people choose which consultants to contact about doing business. While this finding is not new news to any major consulting firm, it provides hard evidence of the value of publications. As a lead generator they are great, serving the same role as, for instance, business conferences. Publish and you will get phone calls. They also are terrific on one's resume; so if you are looking to move on to some other job, they are proof positive that you are an expert on the topic of the book.

Books and monographs play an interesting role in the lives of their writers. Leaving aside the fact that they take up an enormous amount of time, they do several other things. First, if you didn't know a great deal about the topic of the book at the beginning of the process, you will by the time you finish writing it because the project will lead you to read and study about many aspects of the subject. Second, because a book is a finite object, with a specific number of pages, you are forced by the structure of what a book is to organize your thoughts in a logical manner and to articulate them in a way that makes sense to others. The result is, you form opinions about subjects you had not worried about before, and you figure out how best to present your ideas to an audience both in writing and often verbally through presentations. As you have heard, if you want to learn about a topic, teach it; the same applies to books. This is the greatest personal benefit of writing a book. For a company, it improves the intellectual capital of the firm as a whole and, more specifically, that of the participants writing it.

The same benefit does not flow to you if you write an article because, by definition, articles cover only a tiny bit of a subject, whereas a book forces you to look at a topic very widely and in great depth. Articles will help you learn about a topic in an organized manner, but not anywhere to the same degree as will a book. Most people will assume you are an expert on a topic because you wrote an article about it, but once you have written a book, you will understand how much more you really know.

One other by-product of a book is what publishing does to you. To publish, you must at some point push back from your desk and declare "Enough! I am done, it is finished, I want no more of it!" By ending it, sending the manuscript off to the publisher, you force yourself to declare victory, to decide you have said your piece, and to move on. If you are still writing and tinkering with the manuscript, your thinking is not final; expression of the book's themes are still subject to change. But by publishing, you actually take a stand, marking off a line in the sand, saying, in effect, "This is what I have to say about the subject!" Taking a stand is hard to do; that is why so many books are never finished, let alone published. Although there are no hard and fast statistics, most publishers will tell you that they believe there are at least three to six manuscripts floating around for every book they publish. Professors probably have a ratio closer to 2 to 1, but they, too, suffer from the same problem.

Curiously, unpublished papers tend to outnumber published articles by some very high margin. It is not uncommon in business circles for people to have confidence in writing white papers but little or no knowledge about how to publish in a magazine, let alone the courage to approach an editor. You can find business people with 3, 5, 10, or more papers or presentations just sitting in their files that would make wonderful articles or the basis of a book!

VIDEOS, CDS, AND OTHER ELECTRONIC PUBLICATIONS

Life is complicated—long gone are the days when publication meant simply articles or books. Videos, CDs, and white papers on the Internet are simply other channels of communication. The same people who write articles and books often publish with these channels. For example, Robert S. Kaplan, a Harvard Business School professor, is well recognized as an expert on performance measurements. He has published articles and a book on the subject and, within the last several years, he has made videos in which he discusses the same topics. Michael Hammer is best known as the coauthor of the widely read book *Reengineering the Corporation*; he has produced videos on the same subject and uses them in his seminars. Often, videos will be filmed by a company for use in training employees on a topic. Sometimes, these videos then are sold commercially, often by niche publishers who may also sell books. For example, the American Society for Quality (ASQ) sells training videos on quality management practices, and the Computer Channel markets videos on information technology themes. Videos are becoming increasingly popular.

Should you make one? If you are in a training function within your company, videos probably make very good sense so that you can quickly reach many employees. If you want to go commercial, I hope you look good on film! Verbal communication skills are critical in videos, as are the same skills for organizing information as needed for an article or book. It doesn't hurt to have a TV personality, too. While you don't have to be a Dave Letterman or a Jay Leno, or even a Tom Peters, some people just sound awful on tape and need to stick with the written word! So, presentation style is a major consideration when electing to do a video.

People often ask, How long should a video be? Most videos on business topics run anywhere from 15-30 minutes to 45-60 minutes. When done professionally, a video takes about a day of recording to get 30 to 45 minutes, sometimes two days to get 60 minutes of material. You will repeat portions so that the production department or subcontractor to your company can splice the best of you together and add all the graphics, music, and credits. Videos really do take a lot of time to put together. However, once they are taped, you can roll the material onto CDs and the Internet, much like rolling pages of manuscript from earlier works into chapters of future books.

When is it better to use videos over paper documents? Training presentations are the most obvious. But videos can accompany technical manuals, adding explanatory comments to publications, just as Kaplan and Hammer have done. Videos are useful if you are running training programs where you are testing out your ideas for future articles and books to see how the audience responds to your ideas. Videos can be shown at conferences that you do not attend or at meetings where your good communication skills shine most in voice rather than in print.

CDs tend to be less used today, except as training vehicles. That may change in time as more articles and books are published in CD format and as more readers include the necessary technology in their PCs. Almost every major publisher of business books in North America is already publishing in this format or is trying to figure out how to do so. You can find large works of references, such as multi-volume encyclopedias and bodies of laws and government regulations, on CDs. This format is working out very well. Producing these types of publications remains complicated, particularly if text is accompanied by still and motion pictures. In a printed page of an encyclopedia, you might have written a paragraph on Martin Luther King's "I have a dream" speech, but on CD you would also want to include a news clip of him delivering a piece of it. So your workload increases, along with complexity, but also the richness and variety can lead to wonderful improvements in quality. Most work with CD and video formats is done in context with work at your company. There are fewer lone wolves operating here than you see with articles or books because these electronically and digitally based publications require a broad array of talented people (e.g., film technicians, producers) and not just simply one person at a word processor. And, they can be many times more expensive to produce and even publish than paper-based publications.

Then there is the Internet, the subject of much attention and hype. However, there are now somewhere between 10 and 35 million users just in North America, and many more around the world. So it is no surprise that people are putting material out on the Internet. Typically these publications are:

- White papers
- Articles after they have been published in a journal or magazine
- Specially written papers with video and/or sound
- Newsletter-type announcements
- Occasionally, a book

These all can be found at pages reached by searching by author, subject, or title. Often, companies will attach to their web site white papers to stimulate interest in having people contact them as leads for business. Other people put papers out on "the Net" in order to reach out to other experts either to engage in an exchange of information or to debate an issue. There is today almost no topic of interest to a business writer not represented on the Internet. The amount of material available is colossal.

There is good and bad news with the Internet. The good news is, you can reach a lot of people quickly, especially with a white paper, if they can find you. The bad news is, today you have weak copyright protection, so anybody can copy what you have out there and not give you credit for it. They can even change what you said and ship it back out under your name! Many authors are finding it practical to conduct dialogs and research on the Internet but to publish their writings in a paper format. That situation will probably change once we have collectively figured out how to protect intellectual property rights and ensure that authors and publishers can make money from the technology. Right now, however, it is like the Wild West—anything goes that you can get away with!

The final type of publication worth at least mentioning is cassette tape. You have noticed that you no longer have to read Tom Peters; you can listen to him in your car. The same is true for Steven Covey. However, typically the only people who are published on tape, reading their books or discussing their ideas, are nationally recognized celebrities, Second, they also are very good verbal communicators, in other words, they sound great on tape! This form of communication is thus limited today to a tiny segment of the publishing world even though it is really easy to just talk into a tape recorder. Most publishers won't invest in a tape unless you are an established and highly recognized author, which means the vast majority of us really do not have tape publication as a viable option.

Types of Brick Buildings

Walk the streets of old Boston with their three- and four-story colonial buildings grandly sitting next to each other, made out of red brick. The same kind of brick was used to build all those little one- and two-story colonial homes in Williamsburg, capital of the Virginia Colony in the same eighteenth century. Both are wonderful examples of a broad variety of structures that could be built with brick.

The tall buildings in Boston took advantage of limited space and a growing city; the short buildings in Williamsburg exploited greater space and a smaller population. Because homeowners all over the world long ago learned that having dry basements meant they had to keep water away from the foundation, they tumbled across the concept of the dry well—a hole dug underground near the house, into which downspouts could pour their rain water and which they filled with water-absorbing substances, bricks, for centuries. It worked. Go to some of the attractive malls in the United States or to some of the greatest cities of Europe, and you find the sidewalks are made of brick—red, white, black, brown, blue, green, and yellow brick. Bricks everywhere. Walkways of brick are attractive, are easy to lay and replace, and are relatively inexpensive.

The point is, the humble little brick is used in many ways for many reasons. Bricks provide shelter, keep dogs in yards, keep your shoes free from mud, serve as foundations for buildings, draw water away from them all. The masterful builder asks, What do I have to build? What is the best construction medium to do the job? He knows that the bricklayer, once he understands the objective, will know how to do the job. Like the writer, the bricklayer will know what tools to use, will select the right kind of brick, and will calculate the right number to lay. Like the writer, he will worry about the quality of his work, did he lay enough or too many bricks, and do they do the job? Like the writer, the bricklayer will spend time choosing what to build before rushing forward to lay bricks. He knows that sidewalks serve one purpose, walls another, buildings yet a third. Each has its role, requires slightly different construction skills. As a young apprentice, the new bricklayer would have been taught all the different types of bricklaying projects he would be expected to work on once certified in his profession. The master bricklayer would have told him of the different types, when to use them, and how to work in each situation. Like the writer, the master bricklayer could look back on a career filled with many projects ranging from fixing old brick walls to building homes and offices, flower planters and walkways, post offices and country churches. So, the young apprentice must understand the types of projects he might become involved in and why, and not simply how to mix cement or wield a trowel.

$\mathbf{S}$UMMARY

There are many ways to publish. Companies are increasingly using a variety of publishing mechanisms to get their messages out. As we become a services- and knowledge-based economy, you can expect to see more publications surfacing from companies. Individuals often publish on their own or as part of their job. When it is part of a job, companies are developing strategies for publishing (the subject of our last chapters). The publications support more traditional corporate marketing strategies; look at this as another channel of distribution or communications. Often, a firm uses a combination of publishing approaches: articles and books, videos and monographs, all published at the same time on similar topics by the same organization.

In terms of time commitment and degree of difficulty, it goes like this: white paper to article, then come monographs and books, followed by videos and CDs. Any combination increases complexity and probably also effectiveness. If you are interested in only the occasional publication, articles are the best, possibly even a book. If you are serious about communicating in volume, then multiple articles followed by various types of publications are critical. For knowledge-intensive services, such as consulting, this is big business. The top management-consulting firms routinely publish in every medium, usually out-producing the professors themselves! Prolific writers all use a variety of media as well, and for the same reasons.

We have discussed the various types of publications. Now, we have to turn our attention to how to publish. The next chapter is a tactical one, devoted to answering the most widely asked questions in business circles about publishing. While our focus will be on articles and books because those are what most writers publish, my comments also apply to electronic-based publications. So, let's move from "I want to publish" to getting the project done!

4

How to Publish Articles: Some Rules of the Road

. . . .

Publish and be damned.

– Duke of Wellington, 1850s

his chapter presents rules of the road on what to publish, who does it, and how. It is a chapter on the strategy of publishing articles, intended both for authors and for corporate communications experts. It also allows you to look behind the publishing curtain to see how magazines and journals find material to publish.

Let's begin with what this chapter is not about. It is not about how to write an article. It is not a lesson in grammar or writing style, although the tone of your text has to be mentioned. It is not filled with little exercises on composition. Now, let's talk about what we have to work on. We have to think of articles, like books and other work activities, as projects: each has a beginning, middle, and end. I use the plural noun because if you are writing one article, you may want to think about a second or a third, and some of the work for those might have to go on while you are writing the first. This chapter is about project management, about efficient use of your time, about getting to the end of the project. By end I mean an article published and sitting on your bookshelf. As a business person, you understand the value of planning, executing well, and reviewing results. That is how we are going to deal with articles. For nice books on grammar and writing style, take a peek at the back of this book, where I list a few good sources.

SELECTING A TOPIC

Normally, about a half-dozen rules are obeyed by prolific writers. The rules are simple but powerful because they all are based on one simple concept: that articles should be an outgrowth of what you do as part of your work. Conversely, if you are managing a publishing initiative for a company, the same concept applies: you want to pick articles related to what your company wants to be known for.

Rule No. 1: *Decide who you want to read your article because that will help you decide what kind of magazines and journals to write for.* Part of the art of picking a journal or magazine to publish in is to have a topic that fits that publication. If you want electrical engineers to read your work, publish in magazines that they read. Odds are they are IEEE publications; all of these carry serious, detailed, technical articles. You will want to pick a topic that fits this kind of outlet. Also, you might talk to editors to find out what kinds of articles people are interested in these days. Today, successful case studies of projects done well and articles on best practices are very popular with business publications. Shorter, rather than longer, articles are, too. Thus a 2,500 word article will often work better than one twice as long. Don't hesitate to ask magazine editors for advice on length and topic; they usually can be very helpful.

Rule No. 2: *Write about what you have personal, first-hand knowledge of.* Everyone likes to publish articles written by an expert; nobody wants to read a paper written by someone who is not. It also turns out that it is easier to write an article about something you know. The style tends to be good, the material better organized, and the scope is kept to a logical size. Also, odds are that you will provide more new news and research results if the article is an outgrowth of your own work. For example, if you conduct training for employees on quality management practices, you might consider writing on training practices or about how people react to new practices growing out of quality management methods. Also, this approach supports the more basic strategy of writing about what your company wants to be known for and about what you think you want to be known for.

Rule No. 3: *Choose topics that are the right scope for an article, not a book.* The problem is always to struggle with how much detail you need to cover a topic versus how long the article can realistically be. For example, if you can write only ten pages, an article describing in detail the history of your company won't fit in that number of pages. On the other hand, an article on how your company came to decide how to get customer feedback on a new product probably would fit. Are there some generic types of articles that you can choose from? It turns out there really are some. Table 4.1 describes these. You can pick the type that you think might work best for your topic. In the table, I list sample topics to stimulate your thinking about what the overall type and organization of an article might be. Once you have picked the type that seems to fit best for you, organize the article so that it fits the length you think it has to be. Anything that you write beyond that is cut or left aside for a second article. That's how you control scope!

Rule No. 4: *Don't be afraid to select two or more different articles to write to cover the subject.* If you are a first-time writer, the thought of publishing more than one article may seem unimaginable. But if you have enough material for one article, then you have enough for two. When you write the first article, you will find that you do have more than you can use in that paper. Suppose you run a telephone call center, where customers call in to settle billing problems, get service, and ask questions. You decide to write an article on how your firm installed new software to help its staff answer questions. Good topic for a paper, covers use of technology, fast customer service, electronic commerce—all excellent things to write about. But you could get into the article and realize that the measures you put in place to track performance are just as important as the software. Write the first article, and then do justice to measurements as the topic deserves.

Table 4.1

Sample Listing of Common Types of Business Articles
List of good and bad things (e.g., Ten Ways to Market on the Internet)
Trends and directions (e.g., How Computers Will Change Quality Management)
Best practices (e.g., Growing Use of Benchmarking in HR Programs)
Studies and surveys (e.g., Supply Chain Management in 100 Firms)
Advice and tips (e.g., Getting the Most from the Use of Coupons)
Case studies (e.g., Corporate Renewal at Xerox)
Techniques (e.g., Using Run Charts to Communicate Process Problems)
Interviews (e.g., Jack Welch Reveals His Secrets of Success)
Issues (e.g., The Growing Problem of Year 2000 in American Corporations)
Points of view (e.g., Why the Internet Is Now Safe to Use)
Advocacy (e.g., How the ASTD Helps Trainers Perform Well)
Catalog-like (e.g., Ten Software Tools to Support Statistical Process Control)
Product descriptions (e.g., SAP and How Companies Use It)

Write a second article on your measurements, how they help, and what your company is going to do next to improve them. Both articles are interesting case studies. Oh yes, publish them in two separate journals so that you can spread the word about your company's good works across a larger audience!

Rule No. 5: *Pick a topic that will not compromise your company.* Sound obvious? Might not be. So here are some obvious qualifiers.

- ◆ Will your article help competition by telling them how you do something or how many you do? In your eagerness to brag about your company's accomplishments, will you say something that will help competition? Examples: announcing earnings before corporate does; explaining who your customers are; describing unannounced products; detailing your marketing plans. Come on, you say, nobody does that. They do. A number of years ago, a major U.S. publisher received a manuscript describing a piece of software that the author of the article had worked on. He thought that by the time the article was published, the software would be announced and so he would have an article out in perfect time. He would have been fired except for the fact that the magazine editor was smart enough to understand that this programmer had written about an unannounced article. On the other hand, if the product development people and marketing in your company want an article to be published as part of the product announcement PR campaign, that's O.K. Timing and intent is everything!

◆ Will your article expose your company's business strategy? In recent years, thousands of people have written articles about how their companies have done wonderful things, such as reengineer processes, expand services, and improve ties to customers. Your competitors read those articles too, and so the question is: Did you give them a piece of information that will make it possible for them to compete against you? When in doubt, ask marketing people in your company what they think and then act accordingly.

◆ Will your article compromise your company's customers? Just as you would not want a vendor providing you with services to necessarily let the rest of the world know that, your company's customers may not want you to give away information that could hurt them with, for example, their competition. Thus, you would not want to write about negotiations for a partnership on some unannounced project, or the deep discount that they got over other companies, or about a process that you reengineered for them that they think makes them competitive in their markets. Professionals will always get permission from their customers if they are going to write about them. So, if you are, for instance, a consultant who wants to write a case study about your last engagement, get your client's full cooperation and support; otherwise, either mask the name (tell your reader that you are doing that) or don't write the article. Most companies will be delighted to get the free publicity, especially if the article is a positive story.

- ◆ Will your article expose the company to legal action? Compromising confidential information from a customer of your company can get the firm in trouble. So, too, would any acknowledgment of violations of regulations, either intentionally admitted or unintentionally exposed. When in doubt, have your company lawyer read your text to see if there is any problem.

- ◆ Will your article give away intellectual capital? If you write a detailed article about how your company performs a service, right down to a cookbook level, readers might no longer need your help, so you lose potential business. Or, you describe a major benchmarking study that you charged clients $50,000 each to participate in, and publish the results, which thousands of companies get without having paid the $50K. How do you think the participants in your study now feel, especially if you gave away competitively sensitive information? This mistake is easy to make because benchmark results make great articles. You just need to figure out how much you can share in print and how much you cannot.

- ◆ Will your article embarrass an employee or a VIP like your CEO? Misquoting somebody, speculating on your company's future activities, or describing an awkward situation or event are obvious examples. As a good rule of thumb, your mother's advice to you as a kid applies here very well: if you can't say something nice about somebody, don't say anything. This is never so true as in print.

A good rule of thumb: if you have any doubts whatsoever, odds are there is a problem. When in doubt, go to the company lawyer, or your manager, or to someone you trust in the firm and get a second opinion. I don't want to scare you away from publishing; just understand that there are some obvious traps you can fall into. Some companies protect themselves and their employees by publishing guidelines on how to publish. They are usually rolled out terribly, making them sound like censorship rules; yet in fact, most are very practical, so use them to guide your work. If you work in a large company, typically the legal or communications department executes the policy. In a small company, it is your boss or the CEO.

Rule No. 6: *Plan on writing more than one article.* If you are using publications to establish your company's presence, expertise, or visibility in a subject area or if you are trying to establish yourself as an expert on a subject, one article just won't do it. You will have to publish more than once each year for many years. But write your articles one by one so they get done, because your regular job will make it difficult to find the time to write them all at once. If you are orchestrating writing of articles by others, say, as part of a product marketing effort, you may want to make a small list of appropriate articles, then talk various employees either into doing them or hiring some ghost writer to get the job done.

So far, we have looked at these issues from the perspective of the author. What about a company's view? If the firm is attempting to share its intellectual capital inside or beyond the company's borders, is anything different? The reality is, no. There may be more people reviewing strategies and manuscripts, lawyers making sure the firm won't be sued, but essentially the rules apply. For very large organizations, propagators of knowledge and data will not face to the same degree the concerns as those publishing outside the walls of the enterprise. Publishing electronically or on paper is a useful way of pushing information out to "the field" in very large enterprises. For example, newsletters long have served this purpose, but as we increase our need for more substantive material, such as that in articles and books, newsletters are not detailed enough. Nor are databases that many employees may not even be aware of, let alone have access to in any convenient manner. There are many times when just publishing the material in paper form and mailing it out to employees makes better sense. The normal conventions about rules of the road generally apply in such a case. By the way, this approach has been used by very large organizations, government agencies, and private corporations for decades. It works. My employer, IBM, is recognized as the second largest publisher in the world; the U.S. Government is the largest. Our catalog of publications would fill over 5,000 pages!

Normally, corporate publications are centered around information on products or methodologies for doing the work of the firm. Once in a while the human resources community publishes on benefits. However, the communications departments of most corporations have played a minor role in stimulating the publication of intellectual capital. Since they grew up in journalism and public relations, they frequently do not have the depth of knowledge of a topic to find the "experts" in the firm and work with them to publish. But for them, several tasks can be very productive. Simply stated, they should do the following:

1. Develop a list of key experts in the firm and make sure they are being used as speakers at conferences.
2. Work with these individuals to find opportunities to place articles, and later, books, in technical and industry journals, then in national publications.
3. Identify those who publish and work with them to promote them further, getting their material published in better outlets and even investing in PR activities to "hype" them. Corporations hate to do that because they prefer hyping the corporate brand or promoting the fame of senior executives. But in a world that increasingly values what you know, publicizing individuals way down on the organization chart increasingly makes more sense. Very few senior vice presidents invent or sell things, folks down the line do that all the time. In a service economy, she who does is the product!

ORGANIZING AND WRITING

Since book projects are more complex, we will have more to discuss about the subject of organizing work in the next chapter. However, good management practices at the article level are also necessary. Articles vary in such length and complexity that the time you spend could vary from two hours all the way to months. These rules of the road are general, but work with all kinds and lengths of articles.

Rule No. 1: *Before you write, decide in your mind what the article is about and who should read it.* Too many people just sit down at a word processor and start composing. Good writers want to make sure that what they write is consistent with what they want to say. Key messages are thought out in advance or even scribbled on paper. This advance work is especially important if, for example, you are writing an article in support of a company product marketing effort or strategy. Ask yourself the following questions:

- What are the key two or three messages I want my reader to remember?
- How should I present my argument or message?
- What tone do I want to take? (e.g., informal, academic, hard-hitting, laid back, etc.)
- Whom do I want to reach?

Rule No. 2: *Do your research, and gather data for the article before you start writing, but remember that you might have to collect more after you put words on paper.* It is always most efficient to have your data and research done before you write. Often, it is the research or thinking about a topic that makes it possible for you to obey Rule No. 1. Researching and writing is an iterative process, with writing leading to unanswered questions and data leading to new twists and turns in your text. So, plan on doing some research after you have started to write, but plan also to have gathered more data than you can use—hey, maybe that leads to a second article!

Rule No. 3: *Try to write a first draft all the way through before you start polishing or doing more research.* This is a very important rule because when you are actually writing, your mind is operating at a higher level of intense awareness of the issues and data being worked with than at any other time. It is also important to have an overall grasp of information and logical presentation of this data.

The flow of the article's material and text has to be even, and the best way to do it is to try laying it all out in one whack. I did that with this chapter, where I first wrote all the rules then went back and expanded upon them, covering each one with a paragraph of detail. If you have a gap in your data or logic, just make note of it and keep plowing forward until you reach the end. For example, in this chapter, I did not have a clear idea of what the large bricklike sidebar should be (but I knew I wanted one), so I just wrote "place sidebar here" as a reminder that I needed to get one, which I did after I had a full draft of the entire chapter on paper.

Rule No. 4: *Polish, polish, polish.* Nobody can write a clean first draft that reads like fine literature. Have you ever had the experience of trying to make a point or argue a case with all your comments in the right order said just perfectly? Of course not. Well, the problem is the same in writing, only worse because bad phrasing and faulty arguments stick out even more. So once you have a draft, go back and clean up the grammar, writing style, add additional data if needed, and just tighten it up. Plan on your text shrinking in size by about 5 percent unless you left out big chunks of information or text. The 5-percent rule is a good indicator of whether or not you have polished the manuscript enough. Shrinking text forces you to focus on the few but mighty sentences, cutting out all the irrelevant material and rambling statements that take away from what you really are trying to say. Polishing usually takes about as much time or more to do than the original draft took to write.

Rule No. 5: *Have people whose opinions you respect read your paper before you send it to an editor.* The urge to get the paper off your desk and to the editor is enormous, but resist the temptation. Just as in Rule No. 1, you want to take the time to get the message right, and this is another quality check. Others will see the paper differently than you, can offer suggestions on how to improve the argument, and can provide additional ammunition. If you find that someone just flat out disagrees with one of your points, you can acknowledge that in the paper and then provide a counter argument, all in one paragraph, thus taking a preemptive strike against critics who will inevitably appear after the paper is published. This tactic also demonstrates balanced judgment on your part because you recognize alternative points of view. I doubt there is a paper in the world that can't be improved by having others read it before publication. By picking readers carefully, you ensure high-quality critiques. You do not have to rely on an editor who may know nothing about the topic or, worse, send it out to someone to critique who is not an expert. In the end, you and your company are responsible for the quality of your article because it has your name on it as author. So protect your brand!

Rule No. 6: *Step back and ask yourself, "Does my article do what I wanted it to do, or can I make it even better?"* If the answer to the first part is no, then fix the article now; if yes, fix it now, too. Even with experts and editors reading it, you may have missed the mark. Once everyone has worked over the paper, let it sit on your desk for a week, then execute this rule. Some authors will draft an article and put it away for months, drag it out, and read it as a very different piece because time and circumstances have changed. Unless an article is time sensitive (that is, if it must be published soon, e.g., at the time a product is introduced), letting it sit for awhile is a good technique for improving its quality. A little aging gives you perspective, enabling you to improve the text.

Rule No. 7: *Be prepared to work with an editor to fine-tune your masterpiece.* Now that the article is in the hands of an editor, expect that individual to suggest changes because he knows what readers want to see. Editors also have a "look and feel" for the journal that your article must conform to. Rarely are they of much use in adding content, but they are great at packaging since that is what they do for a living. Many authors resist input from an editor. Those who work well with editors normally find that future articles are welcome in the same publication.

Many companies today help authors execute these rules of the road in a variety of ways, about which we will have more to say in future chapters. But let's discuss the role of ghost writers. These are professional writers (e.g., professors, journalists, and corporate communications people) who will either write a text that goes out under your name or who can clean up and polish your work. Most books and articles that appear from famous people like movie stars, politicians, and corporate executives are written by ghost writers, many of whom have published in their own names. You still have to do the research, decide on the message and tone, but they can put the words on paper for you. Many business articles today are written by communications staffs as part of normal marketing and branding work done by a company. What these people bring to the table is writing and organizational skills, you bring knowledge and purpose. In the end, if you work with a ghost writer, you can expect the following to have occurred.

◆ The amount of time you devoted to the project will have been the same as or more than if you had written the paper yourself.

◆ The paper will read very well.

◆ You will have learned a great deal about writing.

Many in corporations see ghost writers as silver bullets, the quick fix. They'll hand the writer a pile of presentations, chat with him for an hour and presto! a perfect paper that reflects their perfect opinions. It does not work that way. In fact, it takes more time to write a paper, chapter, or book using a ghost writer than just simply doing it yourself. So why use them? First, they know how to organize publishable material. Second, they know how to write at a level of quality that is suitable for publication. Third, if you don't know how to write, they may be the only way to get something in print. Editors and publishers like ghost writers because they know that the deliverables will be publishable; editors and publishers usually have little concept of what goes on behind the scenes during the writing effort.

You have to put into a ghost writer's head what you know, explain what your ideas are. That takes time. It can mean several interviews, all-day intense interrogations, and your careful perusal of multiple drafts of papers until the writer gets it right. So, you do not save time using ghost writers, you improve the chance to produce a quality document.

Where do you find these people? They advertise, journal editors keep lists, so do communications companies and departments. Get a name, read the writer's previous material, then interview the writer to see if the two of you can work together. Then, negotiate price and type of deliverable (manuscript). This is no different from hiring an individual as a subcontractor in programming, running an event, manufacturing a component, or performing a task.

The most efficient use of ghost writers is in the situation where a business person really wants to attempt writing a piece himself but needs a mentor, then someone to copyedit—clean up—his manuscript, providing the polish discussed earlier. That way, skills are transferred to the original writer, who leverages the time and experience of a real writer. If you are serious about learning to write, this is the path to go. If you just want to crank out intellectual capital, speeches, and brochures, ghost writers have their role. When it comes to a detailed article or book, however, unless they have personal knowledge of the subject being written about, their value begins to decline because you have to explain so much to them.

Who Publishes

A magazine or journal does not publish articles, editors do. They are the people who decide what to publish, how, and when. Often, it is not the general editor listed on the masthead of a journal's copyright page, it is the second or third editor on the list who actually recruits manuscripts. The second group of people who publish are communications departments in companies that asked you to write a paper, which they now either bang out on a photocopier or send off to a printer/publisher to manufacture. Identifying the individual who decides whether or not to publish your piece is key.

Why do we care? We care because the process of deciding what to write, its organization and tone, messages delivered, etc., are profoundly influenced by these editors. The fact is, this process is highly subjective. As you try to execute Rule No. 1, you will often find it useful to discuss ideas with editors. They can help shape your concept for a paper and, as a result, increase the odds that they will publish it after it is written.

FINDING A PUBLISHER

There are lots of books and articles on how to find a publisher, and some of these aids are listed in the back of this book. We can boil all that advice down to several rules of the road and, just as important, link these to what you and your company want to get done.

Rule No. 1: *It is generally a good idea to pick the journal you want to appear in before you decide what article to write.* Besides giving you useful examples of articles typically published by the magazine you selected, it allows you to ask the business question: Will publication in this journal help or hurt my company and promote the reasons for publishing in the first place? If you write an article about how to use conveyor systems in a warehouse but publish the paper in a general business journal not read by people who buy conveyor systems, all you have is a publication but no impact; you missed your audience. Your reputation and that of your company also emerges as a by-product of where to publish; all the more reason to pick your marks very carefully. This rule also helps you decide where not to publish and why. You may have fun publishing a "trends and direction" article in your city's business magazine, but if all your customers are in another country, you just wasted an article.

Rule No. 2: *Discuss article ideas with potential editors before and during the research and writing phases.* They always have in their minds what themes they want to publish on and often maintain what is called an editorial calendar (a list of topics, by issue, they are pursuing). For example, if *Beyond Computing* plans on publishing a series of articles in the November issue on emerging computer technologies, you would not know that in March unless you asked. If you wanted to write an article on an emerging technology and talked to the editor, you would learn about the

November issue and both of you would have talked about what exactly you could do to ensure a fit into that issue. Once you or your company have established contacts with editors, they often will come to you asking for articles.

Really good communications departments in companies will make lists of what magazines and journals they want to see articles appear in and usually maintain a running dialog with the editors of these publications. Much of the dialog centers around the editorial calendar, with the communications person trying to identify opportunities to plug material into specific issues. The communication person, in turn, will either come to subject area experts in the company to commission articles or will take proposed articles from employees and figure out what magazines to submit them to. Remember, all editors are looking for good papers.

Editors worry about pipelines of material. They have to ensure that they have enough articles for every issue of their publication because they have to publish on time. If they have a monthly with 12 articles or a quarterly with 5, they have to come up with 12 articles every month or 5 every quarter. To do that, they have to touch many more manuscripts than they publish. For example, a normal quarterly of a half-dozen articles, or 24 per year, means an editor probably has to have a minimum of 100 articles in various stages of review, revision, acceptance for publication, in process for publication, or rejection. Some highly select journals may reject 10 or 15 articles for every one they publish. Others may have a gap they have not been able to fill for the next issue, when yours comes in and is a perfect fit! So assume nothing other than they need good material.

Rule No. 3: *If a new author, you may want to pick a lesser-known journal just to begin building up a resume of publications before going after Fortune or the Harvard Business Review.* Everyone wants a business article by Peter F. Drucker, but we are not all as famous or as effective as he is. What Dr. Drucker did was to pay his dues over many decades by writing many articles and books. As a result, today he probably could publish his shopping list in any business publication in the world. And we would read it seriously! The point is, editors like to run with authors who work for highly respected organizations (e.g., IBM, Citibank, Harvard University, Wharton School) or with people who are recognized authorities in their field, and, as mentioned in Chapter One, one way to get recognized is to have a string of publications. For new authors, getting published is often more important than where they are published. In the end, you are building credibility.

Rule No. 4: *On the other hand, if you have an article that is perfect for the Harvard Business Review, go for it.* Not everyone who appears in a well-recognized journal is an experienced author. In the final analysis, an editor is going to select a paper that is authoritative, well done, and is a good fit for the journal. If, for their own purposes, an individual or a company has done important work in a subject area that is of interest to an editor, previous exposure will be of less importance. Your communications department can clean up your work. In the early 1990s, for example, Joe Pine was quietly working on the problem of mass customization in manufacturing, now a recognized strategy for producing tailored products as if they were mass produced. When he felt he was ready to discuss this strategy in print, he had no problem being published in the *Harvard Business Review* and in book form by the Harvard Business Press because he was working on a hot topic and had something to say.

Rule No. 5: *The only articles that ever get published are those that were sent to an editor.* If you don't approach an editor with a proposed article, the editor will never have a chance to publish it. If an editor approaches you and you never write and send in the paper you both agreed on, the same condition applies. What a dumb statement! Turns out, it is not; most papers are never published, and most people never talk to an editor. If you want your stuff published, you have to submit it to an editor; so pick up the telephone, then stick the paper in the mail.

Rule No. 6: *Anything can get published, so make sure your paper is ready to appear in print.* Walk into any Barnes & Noble or Borders bookstore and you get the impression that *everyone* except you has a book out. Walk into a university library's reading room and you get the impression that there are thousands of magazines and journals, each full of articles. We have all seen lots of pure junk published. These include articles of a serious nature in your subject area that were poorly written, flat-out wrong, and full of incorrect information. So that should tell you, anybody can get published. The problem is not getting published, it is in getting a paper published that does what you want it to do. Corporate communications experts and authors often forget that fact. Time is limited, so write what is really important to write, do it well, and it will be published.

Rule No. 7: *Once it's in print, that's it, you can't change it.* Closely related to Rule No. 6 is the cast-in-cement phenomenon. When material is published on a piece of paper, what you say in print stays that way. If, for example, you state one opinion and then five years later the exact opposite is true, tough; you can't change the original article, you can only write a new one. Let's use a book example to illustrate the point. A highly regarded commentator on programming, Edward Yourdon, published a really fine book in 1992 called *Decline & Fall of the American Programmer*, in which he argued that U.S. programmers would be replaced with less expensive ones from India and other countries. It never happened; he overstated his case and in 1996 published a book which essentially had to say "oops." Didn't get it quite right (although the author would disagree with my assessment). You can still buy his fine 1992 book, and the text is the same. In his case, the next book was also well written but. . . While recognizing that things change, make sure that you can live with what you write.

Does the Internet represent a special case? Do all the guidelines and circumstances discussed so far apply? Topics remain the same, perhaps the audience too, although that is not clear yet. However, some best practices beginning to emerge are worth keeping in mind. Let's catalog them as a set of rules.

1. Think of your web site as a magazine. People come to see what various things you have, so give them a table of contents. Have a "look and feel" that portrays the image you want of your organization.

2. Give your audience ways to get directly to a piece without having to page through many other documents. Hence the value of icons people can click on.

3. Because screens have a different shape than a printed page, paragraphs need to be shorter (often one to three sentences); footnotes are awkward because of the requirement to move from one screen to another.

4. Documents are easier to work with if they are short; two to four pages often makes sense.

Now for a few warnings. Anything that is in electronic form can be copied and distributed without crediting you, and today there is nothing you can do about it. Your text can also be altered and still be attributed to you. The conclusion you can reach is that complex, sensitive material should probably still be published in print. However, that does not mean you should not use the Internet to get the word out. Today, people increasingly are going to the Internet to get an initial introduction to your firm. Typically, therefore, it is an excellent place to have descriptions of your firm, products and services, addresses and telephone numbers, and small pieces of text that are like free samples of your intellectual capital. It is an excellent place to list other publications of yours or of the firm.

The basic problem with the Internet as a vehicle for getting the word out is its passiveness. It is just out there, and for anybody to be exposed to it, they have to take the initiative to go to the site. This limits your ability to "push" your message toward a particular audience, the way you can with a book or article that is physically present in many places (e.g., bookstores and on someone's table). There are exceptions, of course, such as those sites someone subscribes to, thus receiving updates when you add text. But that pattern is very much the exception today. Despite all the hype about the Internet and the fact that each month hundreds of thousands of new users log on for the first time, we have a long way to go before the Internet becomes the primary vehicle for the delivery of your thoughts to the business community. Paper remains supreme.

That does not mean one should ignore the Internet. Publishers are trying to figure out how to deliver material on the web, authors want to deposit text out there, and we all like to think of it as a repository that someday will have everything we could want that we can download as needed. But we are not there yet. However, begin to experiment, set up your page, and begin placing material in it. Count the "hits" (number of visits to your site), and in time you will rely more on this electronic medium. But just as marketing people think of the Internet as one of several channels of distribution for their products, so too should organizations think of it as a channel for distributing their intellectual capital.

The one big success to all of this is the use of intranets. These are internal networks within a firm that use the infrastructure of the Internet to deliver material. They tend to be secure, accessible only by password. They started out as large electronic file cabinets with excellent indices, but as knowledge management strategies are implemented, companies are beginning to add functions and to rely on the use of intranets for dialog, training, and work. Companies are only now beginning to figure out how to apply knowledge management strategies to the design of processes, but both intranets and the Internet have been thrown into the stew pot as useful tools in support of internal and external knowledge sharing.

Vision, Work, and Pigs

In the two projects that we have been looking at—bricklaying and writing—there are moments of inspiration but mostly days of perspiration. At the beginning of the project there is the inspiration—the cathedral, the serpentine wall, an article, or the *History of the English-Speaking People*. But then there is the reality of spending a few minutes or hours every day, every week, every month, and every year, laying bricks in some methodical manner. Articles can be done as little brick walls built on rare occasions, or they can be many walks, planters, and other decorative bricklaying projects. Regardless of what kind of bricklaying you do, great bricklayers, like good authors, never wait for inspiration or for large blocks of time. Ernest Hemingway wrote only five pages a day, but he did it every day. James Michener, perhaps one of the most popular and certainly one of the most prolific American novelists of this century, once said that all his fat books were anthologies of ten-page stories. In other words, both writers wrote in article-length chunks!

Both bricklayers and authors share yet another trait: each wants something permanent to come out of the work. We all have good ideas, participate in wonderful and influencing conversations, but unless we write them down and distribute them widely, our influence is limited and only momentary. Remember the Three Little Pigs? One built his house out of straw, and so the Big Bad Wolf had no problem blowing that away, along with the pig. The second pig used wood to build his house and, while it was harder for the Big Bad Wolf to knock down, he did it and so that pig became ham sandwiches. The third wanted to hang around, be remembered, and survive the Big Bad Wolf. So he built his house out of brick. Extra effort, solid materials, and a commitment to success made that little pig just like a good bricklayer and a person who influences the thinking and actions of others through the printed word

What the humble bricklayer teaches us is a simple, powerful lesson: If you want to say something that people will pay attention to, publish; if you want to make a difference with the printed word, then lay lots of bricks every week. Or the Big Bad Wolf might throw a brick at you!

SUMMARY

Articles are quicker to write than books, faster to produce than videos and tapes. They tend to be more current, get published faster, and normally reach larger audiences than does any other form of published communication. Multiple articles on the same theme simply expand the audience you reach, so they are an excellent way to communicate with the audience you wish to reach. Articles do not have to take a great deal of time. In fact, once you get comfortable with writing, you may get into the habit of writing an article at the end of each major project or phase in your work life, to serve almost as a final report. That is how some business people wind up with 30, 40, even 100 published articles.

Despite all the articles that are published, editors feel that there is a famine of good material. There just is not enough to go around, and too many editors find that they get papers just in the nick of time. They are constantly hunting for material, so the opportunity to publish has never been greater. They understand why you or your company might want to publish and are willing to work with you.

As companies get smarter about their corporate images and execute branding strategies, they are finding that articles do mold public opinions. Thus, they increasingly encourage employees to publish as part of a broader marketing strategy. We live in an age when intellectual capital, publications, and other forms of information handing affect the success of a company. Publishing is becoming a crucial component of a knowledge management strategy. The age of "informationalizing" products and services is here. So far, after raw advertising, articles represent one of the most effective ways of pushing around information that supports a company's strategy.

5

How to Publish Monographs and Books: Some Rules of the Road

To be a success in business, be daring, be first, be different.

– Henry Marchant

his chapter describes the differences between articles and books, then shows you how to select book projects and deal with publishers. Along the way you will read about how to manage book writing like a project so that you get the book written and published. Publisher's insights on book publishing round out the discussion.

Monographs and books are very different from articles. Managing the process from conception to publishing is also more complicated. These longer publications cover a wider subject, tend to delve more deeply into issues, and require additional research and information to support. On a more personal level, they take more time to put together. From a publisher's point of view, this kind of a project is different from an article in that the investment required to produce such a publication is far greater and takes more resources. Your time is one of the resources, production staff and cash are others that the publisher picks up. All of these translate into economic risk for a publisher, not simply an opportunity for financial rewards. The risk can be very extensive, particularly if an editor decides to print tens of thousands of copies of your book for the initial offering without any sales record to suggest the number is justified. This will happen, for example, if the author is famous (e.g., a well-known CEO). Publishers can control the risk by printing fewer copies at a time and going back to the printer more frequently. But still, there is risk because they all have profit targets to make.

How Monographs and Books Differ From Articles

So, what is a monograph or a book? Simply put, anything larger than an article. A chapter is dependent on other chapters and rarely stands on its own. A monograph could be the length of a chapter but does stand on its own. For example, many consulting firms will publish monographs—publications that are longer than an article but shorter than a book—that deal with some subject in which they claim to have a competency. Fifty- to one-hundred-page monographs are very common and do quite nicely for demonstrating a technique, describing an issue, or proposing a strategy. They can either appear as one extended essay or as two or more little chapters; normally, they are organized with little chapters. The longer the monograph, the more likely it will be organized by chapters.

So, when does a monograph become a book? There are no hard and fast rules, but usually a monograph is a book at over 125 printed pages in length. Professors will call their own research-based books a monograph, but in business we tend to refer to monographs as small booklike publications on very narrow topics. Table 5.1 lists sample topics that might be suitable for a monograph and in the second column indicates how that topic might be a book.

A book tends to cover broader subjects and is far more detailed. Both are normally intended for sale, although in busi-

Table 5.1

Sample Topics Suitable for Monographs and Books	
Monographs	Books
Implementing Balanced Score Cards in Information Processing Organizations	Measuring the Performance of Companies
Techniques for Optimizing Master Production Schedules	Modern Manufacturing Processes
Applying ABC Methods in Process Design	Activity-Based Costing and Modern Accounting Methods
Applying Business Intelligence in the Petroleum Industry	Marketing with Computers
Hiring Practices in the Retail Industry	Hiring and Retaining Employees: The New Corporate Asset
ESR Software Trends	Leveraging Enterprise Systems for Competitive Advantage
How to Publish Articles on Accounting	Author's Guide to Publishing Articles and Books

ness, companies often publish monographs for internal use or as giveaways to customers. User guides to products that are written as management tools often fit into this category. For instance, a manual on how to install a Lotus Notes software package is neither a book nor a monograph, although it may be hundreds of pages in length. On the other hand, if a Lotus Notes employee wrote a 75-page publication on how to use Lotus Notes groupware to improve team-based management practices, then we would have a monograph.

A well-designed monograph and book have some features in common. The most important are:

◆ Chapters are of equal importance without one dominating over another.

◆ Chapters tend to be of equal length, although that is not a hard and fast requirement.

◆ Chapters tend to have more illustrations and charts and graphs today than years ago.

- Chapters usually are designed with three to five subsections that break up the material (e.g., like the subheader for the next section, "Selecting a Topic").

- Chapters are normally longer than articles.

Which brings us back to what differentiates an article from a book. Because articles are shorter than chapters, they have to be very well written, that is, waste no words, do no wandering around a topic. They have to be net and to the point, whereas a chapter allows you more room to discuss an issue in detail, even to ramble around side concerns as part of your treatment of a topic.

Most authors find that when they write books, they also should and do write articles. Suppose you are writing a chapter and you have decided that a topic will only get 7 pages; but as you get into it, you find yourself drafting 20 pages to do justice to the topic. Now what? You have three choices:

- Cut your precious material down to 7 or 10 pages.

- Write a summary of the 10 pages for the chapter.

- Take a piece of the 20 pages and turn that into an article.

Most authors will implement a combination of all three strategies. To begin with, it is not unusual to cut between 5 and 30 percent of your first draft to get it down to fighting shape; everyone does that. Then, you can figure out if there is a subset of the 20 pages that stands on its own; if so, it is a potential article. In that case, you might summarize the article portion of the paper in a paragraph or two for the chapter and simply refer to the paper, once it is published, in a footnote, in the body of the text, or in a bibliography at the back of the chapter or book. So nothing has to go to waste! Table 5.2, a summary of the differences between books and articles, is a nice checklist to use when selecting topics for publication.

Table 5.2

Differences Between Articles and Books	
Books	**Articles**
Chapters are longer than articles	Shorter; therefore, more tightly written
Cover topics at great length	Topics are very specific, often just one
May take years to write	Usually take days or weeks to write
The source of many articles	Rarely the inspiration for a book
Have limited circulation	Can have massive circulation
Establish credibility	Generate interest
Should be done after writing articles	Good training for writing books

SELECTING A TOPIC

People in business tend to have no problem selecting a topic for a book at a very general level. If someone wants to write a book, it is typically on a topic related to that person's work. A plant manager might want to write a book on managing a highly automated factory, and another book on how to run a car manufacturing facility. A consultant wants to write on some methodology used in consulting—remember James Champy and Michael Hammer and their *Reengineering the Corporation* book? They did reengineering for a living. Programming managers want to write project management books, and sales managers want to write the next "how to sell" opus. But ask them to get specific and narrow the topic down to a manageable scope and they turn glassy-eyed.

The problem is that the act of defining what the book is about is a process of narrowing the scope of the book. Take the idea of the how-to-sell book. What should go in it? Chapters on selling techniques? What about customer relationship strategies? What role should marketing considerations play? Should the discussion involve just selling Girl Scout cookies, or is there a different approach for computer salesmen? Should the comments in the book be directed to sales representatives or clerks at Wal-Mart? By the time this poor potential author has sorted out those issues, you might find that what he or she really wants to write is a book called "Ten Techniques for Selling Commercial Real Estate." Now you potentially run into the problem of having narrowed the scope too much, thus limiting the number of possible buyers who might be interested in the book. A little more work and this author might have decided on the following: "Selling Techniques for Real Estate Agents." Now are included those who sell houses, homeowners who want to try doing it without an agent, and buyers interested in knowing what they are facing.

What criteria should you use in selecting a topic, particularly if it is related to your work? Try answering this list of questions to help you decide:

- Will the book draw more customers to my company, and if so, how and why? A book written by an IBMer about computers may draw a larger reading audience than the same book authored by a Catholic priest.

- Will the book give away company insights that will help my competitors? This is a real issue because most authors want to throw everything they know about a topic into the book. If you write a book detailing exactly every little thing that has to be done on how to write a book, you won't need to come visit me for additional advice!

- What can I write that will give my readers information but not so much that they do not need to come to me any more? This is a variation of the previous question in that what you are usually looking for is a way of increasing a reader's dependence on you. When Steven King writes a novel in serial form, you become dependent on him for more chapters and thus you will buy whatever publication has the sequel chapters.

- Is it a book that has a sufficiently large potential audience to interest a publisher or that is worth my time to do? If the book would be of interest to only a few hundred people, forget it; let some professor write the monograph on the topic. You are looking for exposure. Working with a publisher, you should be able to identify the size of a potential audience. Go for a readership of 5,000 or more for a book or over 1,000 for a monograph aimed at your existing or potential customers.

- Can I, or my company, make money on the book? Or do we just want it as a fat calling card that brings prestige to the firm and credibility to its author? Doing it for prestige is fine because you establish your reputation as proficient in doing whatever the book is about. That can be worth millions of dollars in sales and services. Most books in business are written for this purpose. But if you want to make a living off your books, like Tom Peters, then you write on topics of mass appeal and get on the lecture circuit to drive up sales. The point is, decide *before* you settle on a topic. Too many authors don't face the issue until after publication.

- Will I have anything important or new to say? It helps to have something new to say or a different way of saying something old so that it resonates well with the reader. Each year dozens of books come out on how to manage information technology; books on that subject have been published since the 1950s. But each new one is fresh because the examples are of current computer technology and the case studies are of things people are doing at the time of publication. If you have new ideas, like George Stalk did when he wrote a book on cycle time reduction, then you are in good shape. Often, unique projects represent bodies of work that, if written down in books, represent good sources of new ideas of relevance to potential readers.

- How does this book align strategically with what I personally want to get done and what my company is attempting to do? Good question. Often, it is never asked or answered. If your company wants recognition as the world's best in benchmarking, like Xerox Corporation does, you publish articles and books on benchmarking. Xerox employees, for example, published nearly a dozen books on the topic. The book is simply another form of marketing and advertising or, to use a fashionable term of the 1990s, credentialling.

♦ What is the best approach for reaching my intended audience? In fact, who is my intended audience? Understanding who would read your book helps you make many decisions related to the organization and style of the book. If the audience is academic, you may opt for a scholarly tome complete with footnotes and large vocabulary. If the audience is general management, it better be around 300 pages and have a light, fast-paced style. Forget the footnotes! What would your customers read? Ask them. Ask a publisher or another author in the subject area of your potential book. This may be a key issue for the publisher.

Having said that, are there some best practices for getting effective ideas for books and articles? Want a book that people will read? Usually, the following strategies will get you to a good topic.

♦ Get ideas on topics from publishers before you start outlining.

♦ Write about what you know because that probably means you know what is needed.

♦ Fill a need; we don't need another book on "How to Use a PC."

♦ Don't write a book publishers won't publish. What?! Yes, some people will write a book, thinking humankind needs it, without validating the need for it. Mighty risky strategy!

♦ Remember, it has your name on the cover, so don't pick a topic that will embarrass you later.

♦ Keep it short; this is not the time to write a 20-volume encyclopedia.

♦ Target your audience as widely as possible because that gets you more readers, more sales.

Are there some perennial hot business topics always in fashion? If you look at what gets published, the answer is yes. Here's my list. Can you add to it?

- ◆ "How to" management books because people want to implement; they are impatient with theory
- ◆ Case studies and war stories because these are popular, believable, and effective
- ◆ Change management because it usually is the biggest topic on the minds of senior executives, most consultants, and many business and engineering professors and professionals
- ◆ Industry and functional trends because change is rapid and risky, causing people to find ways to survive this churn and chaos and make sense out of it all
- ◆ Detailed technical "how to" because this is a skills development issue (e.g., look at all the Dummy books on computing)
- ◆ Productivity and efficiency because the topic never goes away
- ◆ New and emerging strategies because everyone is afraid the other person will get ahead

You can think of other criteria but the point is made: although the topic is important, why it is so and to what purpose you will put the project is even more significant. As you address those issues, you may need to write several outlines of the book as you wrestle with the riddle of which approach will be the most effective for you, your company, and your customers (readers).

I suggested earlier that you might have multiple outlines for a project before settling on one. Here is my technique for settling on one outline that has the right scope, the right fit for the audience, and that reflects what I really want to get done. My technique makes it possible then to treat writing a book not as a literary exercise but as a project, just like any other you do in business.

Step I: *Take out a sheet of paper and write down a working title for your proposed book; worry about the cute title after you have* *written it.* Write your name under the title of the book so you begin to visualize what this book is about and by whom.

Step 2: *Take out a second sheet of paper and write down the titles of the table of contents for this book just like you would see them in a printed book.* Imagine the ideal book you would want to buy on this topic. If you are going to have seven chapters, then you have seven lines on this page numbered 1 through 7. Stare at it, make sure it contains all the chapters you want, and in your mind ensure the chapters generally would be of roughly the same importance and same length.

Step 3: *Now, under each chapter heading, add three to four bullets that have three to five words describing what that part of the chapter is all about.* Put the list away for a day or two, then stare at it again. You will find you need to add others. Use the table of contents of this book you are reading as an example of a table and then the subheadings of this chapter as examples of subheadings. I think by know you know where I am taking you.

Step 4: *Once you have fiddled with the more detailed table of contents, write a paragraph under each chapter and before the sub-headings, describing what you think this chapter is all about.* Use my first paragraph of any chapter or the short descriptor above that text (and below the quote) as examples of what to write. Put the text away for several days, then come back and stew over it to make sure you don't need to add or subtract material from it.

 Step 5: *Now write a draft of a preface (ideally three to seven double-spaced typed pages) that describes what the book is about, who should read it and why, and what your key messages are.* Forget that you don't have any acknowledgments to make (normally put in a preface) at this point. Read the prefaces of any two or three other business books to get a drift of what goes into these little essays. This exercise ensures that you have put a reasonable fence around the project and can explain it. Once your draft preface is done, compare it to your table of contents, fix the inconsistencies, and put the whole thing away for several more days. Then look at it again, and make changes if appropriate.

Step 6: *Show your document to several colleagues, managers, etc., to get their input on organization, scope, and content.* Incorporate the best of their ideas into it. Now you have two wonderful things in a short document:

- a clear idea of what this book is going to be about and probably its length
- half of a book proposal already drafted for a publisher

 You are ready to get started turning this into a project with the real possibility that it would be done!

What happens if you go through this little process and you are not happy with it? Do it again. It is a process that takes only about two hours to do. You can come up with several versions of the topic for a book, testing to see which is a better fit for what you want to get done and what works for others, such as publishers. You could, for example, come up with an outline for a short or long book on your theme. Or, you could have an outline of chapters describing a subject and another that is a collection of chapter-length case studies, or yet a third that is a combination of narrative, case studies, and extensive display of tools and techniques.

Better to spend the time up front playing with these outlines and approaches than later because it takes more time to rewrite a book than to organize your thoughts in the beginning. The quality of the book also increases, and you stay focused on your original intent. Does that mean you will not change the book? Probably every book that was ever written wound up being different from what the author began with. However, you want to minimize churn. The outline helps, yet you want to accept changes in concept too. Any proposed changes can at least be accepted or rejected to the extent that they support or contradict the purpose of your book.

We live in an age of lists. They are quick to read, often summarize a lot of information, and can stimulate thinking. So, if you need a list of ten things to do and to keep in mind to really get a book written, this might be it:

1. Picture in your mind the title, table of contents, and length of the book.

2. Expand your table of contents as described above and imagine what illustrations, charts, and graphs you might have in it.

3. Treat your first draft of the preface as if you were writing a book review.

4. Show your outline to experts, colleagues, and publishers to see if it makes sense.

5. Put the outline away for a month and then come back to see if it still makes sense to you; if not, redo it or tune it up.

6. Then, act like a project leader by putting together your work plan with dates for doing research, writing, reviewing and critiquing activities by others, and for developing a marketing plan to sell the book to a publisher.

7. Write the book, planning on many long weekends, or get someone to ghost write the thing for you, but still plan on many hours of reviewing. You want to make sure it says what you want it to.

8. Warning: The book will take twice as long to write as you planned.

9. Editors are good people; seek their advice all along the way.

10. When you have come to hate the manuscript, it is ready to be published.

Organizing and Writing

Most people do not write books, and many authors who have published books will tell you that they can't write books! So what gives? Keeping a large book in your head and coordinating all its various parts is very difficult to do. The key is organization and sound business project management. While I do not want to teach you project management in this book, there are some principles we use in business that are directly applicable here. Four very effective ones are:

1. Keep lists of "to do's" by chapter, by time, by topic.

2. Break down your book into chunks of work, just as you would any project.

3. Worry about that portion of the project you are working on now.

4. Set deadlines for getting tasks done. Then stick to them!

What do these principles mean? Lists of actions that need to be done at the data gathering or writing stages are helpful. These could be as simple as photocopying material for use in a chapter or for plugging in data in the text. Remember when I said to break each chapter outline into several segments? Breaking work down into chunks applies here. It turns out, most people can't write a 20- or 50-page chapter, but just about anybody can write 7 to 10 pages—a good length for a typical subheading in a chapter. So worry about writing only those 7 to 10 pages, then the next 7 to 10 pages, and so on until they are all done for the chapter. Then write an introductory section to the chapter if you did not already do so and, next, a summary paragraph or page that pulls together all the ideas from the various sections in the chapter. That is chunking the work down into manageable portions. Do that for every chapter until the book is done.

Deadlines work in business and they work with book projects. Break down the research and data-gathering activities into chunks, organize folders to hold material for each chapter, and then set deadlines for completion of the basic research, chapter by chapter. Then, set deadlines for when you will complete drafts of each subheading of a chapter or for the whole chapter. For example, I try to write a chapter every six weeks, which means I have to draft a subsection about every 10 to 14 days. If I am ahead, great; if I fall behind, I have to spend more time on it this weekend to catch up.

Don't wait for inspiration or the right time, just break the work down into pieces and keep doing something all the time. Remember our bricklayer.

What about inspiration, what role does it play? Prolific writers rarely see it. Instead, they talk about continuous production. Psychologically, they do several things:

- They attempt to work at the same time each week, year in and year out. I personally write every Saturday and Sunday morning before my family is up and around.

- They write in the same room, such as an office at home, so that whenever they are in that room, their mind immediately and subconsciously knows what it must do, which is to work on the book.

- They do the same amount of work each time and then stop. Remember Ernest Hemingway's practice of drafting five pages each day and then going off to seek the adventures we have all read about? How do you think James Michener got all those fat novels written? Talk to prolific writers of business books and they will tell you the same. Even people who only publish one book or even one article a year tend to mimic the same pattern of behavior.

Often, new authors and even some experienced ones will ask: Where should I start writing the book? Chapter One? Anywhere? The Conclusion? The toughest chapters to write are the first and the last. The first requires that you know what the whole book is about in order to set up your audience; the last brings it all together, silhouetting our hero against the sunset. Start with Chapter One, knowing that you will have to rewrite significant portions of it later, as a way of getting your feet wet. Then, write chapters in sequential order if at all possible, all the way to the last. Then clean up Chapter One. If your book has only one real great chapter and everything else is foreplay and aftermath, then write that one first. Yes, you would be surprised how many business books really have only one or two important chapters!

One editor taught me a trick that most people forget to implement. He told me that no reader is required to read your book in the order in which you wrote it. Nor do they have to read all of it. Therefore, if you really care to have someone read your book, begin each chapter with a brief description of the chapter and why it is important. Set it in context. Always end your chapters with a statement on the significance of the material and on what the next chapter is about and why we (you and the reader) have to go there next. In other words, don't forget to persuade your reader to continue reading your stuff.

A very recent development in the area of digital publishing can have profound effects on an author or a corporation implementing publishing programs. Increasingly, the major publishers, such as Prentice Hall and McGraw-Hill, are rapidly acquiring important skills in the creation of digital products and in the marketing of these. Essentially, the way it works is that an author produces a manuscript, say, with 15 chapters. The publisher prints a book—just as always—but then makes available one of three types of additional products drawn from the same material:

- Individual chapters as stand-alone products (both electronic or in print)

- Electronic versions of the original book

- Printed or electronic combinations of various chapters from different books

In other words, intellectual capital is being repackaged in new ways today. As you and your organization think about publishing, it is not too early to start thinking about the implications of repackaged publications, both electronic and paper. In time, the electronic version will be enhanced with video that has obvious advantages over straight text in teaching and bringing subjects "to life."

From your perspective as the author, if the unit of intellectual capital is the chapter, then you would want to make sure that all chapters are comprehensive, that is, that they can stand on their own with minimal or no literary surgery. This means asking yourself the question, "Does this chapter say everything I want to cover on the topic of the chapter?" That means also not constantly referring to material in other chapters, even at the risk of some repetition. It might even mean that you have to discuss with a publisher or manager of a knowledge network what software tools you should use for the text and graphics employed in preparing a manuscript.

FINDING A PUBLISHER

There is a secret all new writers need to learn and that all experienced authors know: book publishers are always looking for new material. In fact, they will admit it! A book to a publisher is a product—no product, no sales; good product, lots of sales. You, as an author, are the developer of new products. The big concern that publishers always have is, will you develop a product, and is it any good? You must deal with those two issues, both of which are not precise or easy to explain.

There are many books on how to get your stuff published. The advice always boils down to several actions:

- Develop an outline and proposal.
- Talk to a publisher about who the audience is and why the book will sell.
- Pick publishers who publish on the same general topic as your book.
- Then deliver the manuscript.

Table 5.3 illustrates the kinds of questions a publisher will ask when determining whether to take you on. The issues are essentially the same from one firm to another. The process is essentially the same as we reviewed in Chapter 4 so there is no need to cover the same ground.

There are some differences. Here are some rules of the road to follow that will help.

Rule No. 1: *Don't waste an editor's time unless you are serious; too many people who talk to editors are not committed.* Everyone seems to be floating ideas about books, so make sure that you have done enough homework to get an editor's attention.

Rule No. 2: *Let an acquisition editor work with you to craft the outline; they then share ownership of the idea and success of the project.* They usually have good ideas because they see many book proposals and they work in the book market.

Rule No. 3: *Always prepare a good outline and, if necessary, sample chapters, to convince the publisher you can do the job and are committed.*

Table 5.3

Key Questions an Editor Will Ask an Author
Who is the audience?
In one short paragraph, describe your book.
What are the three key "bullet points" that will really sell your book?
Do you have anything new or important to say?
Does the book have a point of view?
Have you written before?
What are your credentials for writing this book?
Would you rate yourself as a world class authority on the subject? Some publishers never know what a gem they have, so make sure they do!
What is your competition and why is your book better?
How many pages is the work?
What prerequisite knowledge is required?
Are you going to meet your schedule?
Are there time or personal commitments that will interfere with your schedule?
How flexible are you in responding to changes, criticism, etc…?
Are there potential permission issues that may interfere with electronic or subsidiary rights?
Is there any possibility of special or corporate sales?

Rule No. 4: *Meet your deadlines and so surprise your editor; editors know the old Biblical phrase, "many are called but few are chosen."* They assume you will miss your deadlines, maybe not even write the book, so surprise them by doing what you said you would, and on time.

Rule No. 5: *Avoid writing the book and then finding a publisher unless you are already a well-established author.* If you wait too long, it becomes nearly impossible or unreasonable to make changes to make a publisher happy if you got it wrong in the first place (like you wrote a 600-page book when one only 250 pages in length would have been ideal).

Rule No. 6: *Don't be a pig when negotiating contracts; publishing is not always a high-margin business.*

Rule No. 7: *Once your book manuscript is in the process of being produced, don't fight the production department; they are worse than the government.* They have their way of doing things and if you try to change that, they will ignore you or simply delay publication of your book.

Rule No. 8: *You had better plan on offering to help market your book because publishers are notorious for doing a poor job in selling more copies than are necessary for their normal profit targets.* We will deal with this problem in more detail in the next chapter.

Rule No. 9: *Remember that your text is a cathedral under construction and can and should be constantly improved.* If you want fine art, go paint a picture. Until it is published, use every opportunity to polish and tune the manuscript and be open to suggestions for improvements from many sources.

Rule No. 10: *Be realistic about how many copies of your book can be sold; your editor normally is.* Very few books become best sellers. In the United States, for example, less than three dozen books qualify as best sellers each year. Very few business books, for instance, make *The New York Times* Best Seller list.

What to Include in Your Chapters

- Give a chapter a title that tells the reader what it is about. Cute titles irritate business book readers. Remember, this is not a novel for entertainment. You may be discussing the way a company could become the next Microsoft, so don't mislead your readers.
- Tell people what the chapter is about, up front, in page one, paragraph one of every chapter.
- Flip-flop back and forth between concepts and ideas on the one hand and real-life examples on the other. Fill the chapter back and forth; one type of text helps the other.
- End the chapter with a summary of what you think are the key take-aways. Don't assume your poor readers can arrive at that all by themselves—you may be a lousy writer.

1. You never wrote it in the first place.
2. You took too long to write it.
3. You never had a clear idea of what it was about.
4. You failed to make sure publishers wanted it.
5. You didn't invest the time, sweat, and energy into it.
6. You waited for inspiration.
7. You experienced Murphy's Law.
8. You didn't really want to write it.
9. You took the manuscript reviewers too seriously.
10. You picked a lousy publisher.

SUMMARY

If there is a central message in this chapter, it is to treat writing not as a form of literary adventure but as you would any business project. Justify it the same way, commit time the same way. And always have good business reasons for the book and what you do. But don't take my word for it. Read what Herb Addison, the highly experienced business book acquisition editor at Oxford University Press, says:

> Practicing managers have an opportunity cost when they pick up a business book. Put bluntly, it has to be worth their time to read it. If it is not, they will not read it, and they will not recommend it to peers. Business books sell as much by word of mouth as by advertising. Therefore, always be aware of the practical application of the material you are writing about.

He often reminds authors that:

> Books like these should be clearly about something of vital interest to the practicing manager. It may not always be obvious what this is, even to the author. A book on information strategies may really be about organizational transformation, or about listening to one's cus-

tomers, or about changing corporate cultures. It would be good to decide early on what a book is to be about.

He always reminds authors that every book should have themes that bind the chapters together. I would also add, don't forget the few and mighty messages you want your reader to walk away with. The message should always focus on what can be applied. Avoid telling us how you did research, just share the results and what it means to the reader. Herb Addison has taught many authors the old trick about getting a reader to move with you through the book: "A 'kicker' sentence at the very end to entice the reader into reading the next chapter. Use your imagination." How about: "If the problems that these companies faced were difficult, they were easy compared to those we describe in the next chapter"?

My hook for the next chapter: If you thought figuring out how to get a book organized was hard, wait until you see the problems writers in the business world face with copyright permissions, the rights and rules your employer has, and what happens if you have to get other authors to be as enthusiastic in getting their work done as you are! These are the topics of the next chapter. In fact, it is the most important chapter you can read since Chapter One!

6

Special Issues of Publishing in a Business Environment

Coming together is a beginning. Keeping together is progress.
Working together is success.

– Henry Ford

This chapter focuses on the publishing environment in business, which has special problems and requirements that I explore below. These include issues of copyright ownership, who gets the royalties, and how best to avoid problems while encouraging publishing by employees. I end with a brief discussion of mentoring for publication.

One of the basic premises of this book is that writing and publishing within a business environment is different than in higher education. The essential differences stem from the fact that businesses and most government agencies do not have research and writing missions as a core duty. Professors do, and as a result they have much of the infrastructure, culture, and reward systems needed to facilitate publication. Businesses do not offer such things, even though today there is growing interest in having employees publish. Before we can have any discussion about what corporations can do to facilitate publication, the key issues they face, along with authors, need to be understood.

The issues are serious enough. Employees would rather not write for publication than risk being fired for printing something that some executive way over in another part of the company gets upset with. Historically, corporations have built complex process and policy fences around employees to keep them at arm's length from newspapers, radios, and TV. In every major corporation you know of, we hear of someone getting fired each year for saying something to the press that some executive thought should not have been said. Corporate lawyers have developed elegant procedures that essentially declare that anything in an employee's head belongs to the company and cannot be shared outside the firm without going through some onerous review process. Violators are routinely fired quickly. Employees do not have the protections for expression that professors enjoy. So, in short, all the signals we have grown up with suggest that publishing carries risk with it. There are many related issues, some of which we will discuss below. Changing many of these long-standing practices will become essential if a firm is going to take publishing seriously. It takes only one incident to make employees run for cover. On the other hand, a couple of good role models can stimulate much positive emulation.

WHO OWNS THE INTELLECTUAL CAPITAL?

Let's begin with the most basic issue of all: Who owns the intellectual capital in your head? A brief lesson in copyright laws can help answer the question. Most countries around the world have laws that protect authors from others publishing their work without their permission. While enforcement of these laws varies widely, in the United States both the U.S. Congress and the courts have worked diligently to protect these rights. As a normal rule, copyright laws protect an original expression of an idea that appears in print, a video, movie or television program, on disk, and in other electronic and visual media. What these laws do not protect is the original idea, only how you express it. Patents, on the other hand, which are different from copyright laws, protect the idea or thing. Copyrights protect expressions of ideas; patents protect ideas and things. Publications are normally copyrighted and inventions are patented.

Let's complicate this just a little more. A technique or way of doing something, such as how you perform a service, can be patented, but the manual that describes this service would be copyrighted. For our purposes, we will worry about copyrights because you don't patent publications.

When most corporations began to worry about rules and regulations for its employees, they focused on patents, then moved on to copyrights. As companies invented and manufactured products, they patented them. As competitors tried to develop knock-off or competitive products, companies sued each other over patent infringements. As a result, patentable activities were made secret, and employees were not allowed to share that knowledge across the company, let alone in print. Very quickly, corporate lawyers began putting fences around copyrights too, since if you wanted to protect patents, you would also want to hide or protect information about what the firm was doing. This was particularly the case with an established corporation and especially true with firms in highly competitive industries.

As a result, unless you work in a young company that has yet to establish a policy on publishing, what most companies will do is to take the position that any ideas or work that you have done on behalf of the company, or related to the "business interests of the company," belong to the firm and are subject to their control. There are firms, for example, that begin the process of control on the first day an employee comes to work by having them sign an application form containing some language that says, in effect, the employee agrees to sign over all rights to the firm for any intellectual capital, ideas, inventions, etc., they come up with related to the firm, sometimes for life and even after leaving the company!

While companies will frequently claim more rights than most authors are willing to acknowledge (and sometimes authors will fight their firm in courts over the issue), the fact is both the corporate legal and communications communities will normally begin dealing with an author with the attitude that the company owns their ideas. Authors begin by bumping into that reality. In practice, issues are not as black and white as a lawyer would like you to believe; gray is a better color. You should look at each publishing situation on a case-by-case basis and be judged by your management and the firm at large that way.

As the issue of intellectual capital has grown in importance during the 1990s, debates about copyrights within corporations increased. Corporations that once did not worry too much about the issue are becoming very protective. Authors who have personal skills and a publishing track record are increasingly becoming irritated with their employer's restrictive practices and will leave the firm; you see this with well-known consultants, for example. Often, they start their own businesses or become professors.

Is there a resolution to the question of who owns the copyright? It depends. However, always ask the question at the time you and a publisher have decided to publish. Normally, the publisher holds the copyright. You, as the author, assign to the publisher your rights to copyright, which allows the publisher to reprint your material in movies, scripts, in a foreign language, and in various electronic forms. However, you could copyright the material and simply allow the publisher the right to publish. Or, you could assign the copyright to your company, giving the publisher the right to publish the material. If you are writing on a topic that grew out of your company work, you probably would have the copyright in the name of the firm, get written permission to authorize the publisher to publish the material, and the publisher would acknowledge the firm's ownership of the material.

The publisher is less interested in who owns the copyright than are companies. What publishers worry about are:

- Will they have the flexibility to publish the material in various ways, reprint, and distribute?
- What is the best way to make money from the publishing venture?
- How will the copyright be managed over the long term?
- Will they be able to prevent anyone else from publishing the exact same material?

Most publishers have in their contracts a clause that says the publishing firm gets a certain percentage of the royalties earned from all editions of the material (e.g., foreign language), while the copyright holder (the author or your employer) normally gets the rest of the royalties.

Let's summarize: If you write about things that were developed on the job, copyright normally belongs to your employer. If you publish on topics marginally related to the firm, then copyright might be yours or the firm's and neither one might really care. But if it is an issue, step one is to discuss the topic with your organization's management and step two, with your company's legal counsel. Lawyers will start by insisting that everything belongs to the firm, and you and your management then work from there to figure out what makes sense for all parties concerned. As companies have moved toward encouraging employees to publish, they have had to revisit their hard and fast guidelines of the past and are developing more flexible ones. Thus, you now see situations where royalties go to authors, and copyrights are held by any of the three parties involved.

Publishers are having as hard a time with business writers as corporations are, although they usually do not admit it. The problem is less with the author and always with the contract. Publishers for over a century have had a fairly standard set of terms and conditions that were designed to define the relations between author and publisher. With the injection of a firm into the now three-way dialog, publishers are having to renegotiate their standard contracts. Few editors have any experience with this, and their lawyers are just beginning to get engaged. Many new issues pop up: royalties, liability clauses, who defends the firm, author, and publisher in a lawsuit, and, of course, language concerning copyright ownership or permissions. But these are being worked out on a case-by-case basis as individual authors and companies approach book publishers. These issues rarely occur with articles or electronic media.

Care and Feeding of Your Company

In addition to discussing copyright issues with corporate lawyers, there are actually more important and less obvious issues to deal with. Copyrights are not terribly complicated issues in normal circumstances. But other issues are of greater concern, such as giving away company secrets or publishing things that embarrass the company. Not to scare you, nonetheless, there are some obvious traps. Table 6.1 lists some of the most common ones.

Table 6.1

Common Publishing Mistakes
Speculating in print about the economic and financial prospects of the company if you are not an officer of the firm. In fact, in the United States it is against the law to discuss financial results before the corporation reports them to the public.
Interpreting corporate policies and practices for which you personally are not responsible.
Describing unannounced products or services currently under development. In the United States, that can get you into legal trouble if it influences how the market reacts to a competitor's products because of your speculations.
Sharing information about who your customers are and data about them without their permission.
Speculating about any future actions your company might take.
Sharing information that would directly benefit your company's competitors.
Commenting on specific individuals in your company, even if your comments are positive.

Now for the positive side of the discussion: What normally can you publish about? Typically, these subjects include:

+ How to use a product or service (e.g., the manual that comes along with your PC printer)
+ Case studies of how to use products or services (e.g., how to fly a specific brand of aircraft in cold weather, written by a pilot working for the manufacturer of that airplane)
+ Your thoughts on an industry or technical issue so long as you speak as an individual, not stating the "official" or perceived "official" position of your firm (e.g., my views on the value of new business measurement techniques)
+ Your thoughts as an "official" statement of the firm, and you state that you speak for the company and with the

firm's permission (e.g., why firms should implement Lotus Notes or what the firm's service strategy is)

- Management of technology and business in general (e.g., on the value of quality management practices in the insurance industry)

- Client projects, provided you received permission to do so both from your firm and the client (e.g., resulting from a consulting engagement)

- Subjects of interest to your company that illustrate your knowledge and that of the firm (e.g., managing restaurant franchises if you are an employee at McDonald's)

- Topics of which you have direct knowledge (e.g., project management, ABC accounting)

There are five questions you can ask yourself to help decide what is publishable and what is not. If any of the answers make you nervous, then go see colleagues, management, or even a company lawyer. A little caution here is very useful because there are many topics you can write about that do not cause problems and, in fact, enhance what you and your company are trying to do. To facilitate the effort, answer the following questions and then go forth and publish.

1. *If you were a competitor of your firm, would you find the information of direct economic benefit to you?* Would it cost your company in lost business or prestige? Would it embarrass the firm or anyone in it? Related to these concerns, would the publication irritate or embarrass your company's customers?

2. *Does the topic leave you with any doubts or concerns?* In other words, are you really not sure? If your little voice inside is talking to you, listen. For example, this happens if you are writing about a product or technique that might, in fact, be the centerpiece of work going on in another division of the company; make that part of the company comfortable with what you want to publish.

3. *How would my management feel about the material?* Happy? Angry? I believe in always making sure my manager knows what I am publishing about and, if he or she is an expert on the subject, I really want feedback anyway. Many managers will want to review your material before publication to make sure no sensitive comments are made. Trust and judgment sometimes are a problem, but if something silly gets published, managers of the authors are also blamed, so it is hard to be too critical of their caution. They, too, are usually new at publishing. Command and control habits, while dangerous to apply around thought leaders, nonetheless are exercised often and show no signs of going away. It is a condition of writing in a business environment. If authors have a problem with that, they may just have to think about becoming professors or independent writers. This sounds harsh, but it is a reality. In many cases, however, managers play a very positive, protective, and encouraging role.

4. *What do experts on the content of your material think?* You should have experts read the stuff anyway just to help you improve it. But begin with experts in your own company or department. That way, you get the double benefit of someone looking at the content to improve it while checking to make sure it won't hurt the firm.

5. *Am I speaking on behalf of myself or the firm?* After the first question, this is the second most important one to answer clearly. Unless you were specifically ordered by your company to write a piece that clearly is a statement of the firm, you should always write in your own voice. If the reader perceives that you are speaking on behalf of the firm, then you have to make changes in the text. For example, in a book's preface you can add a sentence that literally says "this book is the result of my own work and does not represent the expressed or implied views of the XYZ Corporation." Normally, your employer does not want you speaking on behalf of the corporation.

This question is a difficult one because the line is often fuzzy between your voice and that of the company. On the one hand, if you are writing on topics clearly related to your industry, publishers and readers are interested because you are part of that industry and not because you are a person with an opinion. Yet on the other hand, you want to display your own independence. How do you walk the line? You can take several steps.

If you want a close alignment with your employer:

- For a book, get your employer's permission to state up front that this volume reflects the firm's position.
- For a book, you might have a guest introduction written by a company executive—a de facto blessing of the book by the company.
- For an article, weave into the text "we at the XYZ company..."

If you want to keep your distance from your employer:

- State up front that this is an expression of your ideas and not those of the company you work for.
- Base your research and sources on noncompany sources (e.g., such as information found at your local university library and in other secondary material).
- Base some of your research and discussion on material from the company (with permission) and some from noncompany sources (e.g., secondary published material).

Normally, editors of magazines and journals do not concern themselves with whose voice you have written, but book publishers do. It is not uncommon for a book editor to have a discussion with a prospective business author about whose voice is in the book and how best to deal with that. If the book is an expression of the company, the publisher might request written permission from the firm to publish the book because the voice often is the owner of the copyright.

 Which leads us to the question all authors ask: Who gets the royalties? The question does not have a clear answer, but, in practice, several situations occur.

When you wrote at the request of your employer: This is the situation in which your manager asked you to write something at your company's expense, on company time, using company resources. Such a publication is no different from a company-published document. Therefore, royalties would go to the company. A common example of this kind of publication might be a user manual or a book designed to demonstrate the capabilities of the firm or of a product. In this situation, the author is just doing a normal job, which happens to include writing and publishing.

When you wrote on your own: If you perform research on your own time, at your own expense, and used little or no company resources, then royalties would normally go to you because your company would have no practical claim to ownership or intellectual content. For example, if you were a sales manager but wrote textbooks on statistical process control, your company would probably not care, let alone go after control of the copyright or royalties.

When it is not clear: Here, the circumstance is that you write on business topics that relate to your work but you include material you developed on your own time, at your own expense; still, the book might contain some company content. Consultants frequently fall into this category when they not only perform research in the public domain or use published literature but also draw upon their own experiences within the company that employs them (e.g., writing books on project management or on a consulting expertise). In many situations, it becomes difficult to say where the company's content begins and where it ends. Increasingly, as companies recognize the extra effort required of an employee to write, they are letting the employee keep the royalties.

The issue of royalties rarely involves articles, where royalties normally are not paid. But it does involve books, where royalties are always hoped for. It quickly becomes an emotional issue. The lawyers get excited because they are trying to protect the company's assets (even though you probably got formal copyright permission to use company material), while your management generally is delighted to see you publish. You, the author, want to recover research and writing expenses via royalties. What all three parties fail to realize is the triviality of the royalty issue; most books only make several thousands of dollars in royalties, but the costs of researching and writing the tome far exceed that income. In this situation, settle the point up front with your manager and get it in writing in case your manager is gone three years later when the first royalty check floats in!

MULTIPLE AUTHORS

Team-based publishing is becoming very popular in business. This is the situation where multiple authors have their name on the title page or are authors of individual chapters. In the academic world, one author is usually selected as the editor, and it is that person's responsibility to recruit the individual chapter authors and then to mold their various writings into a cohesive volume. It is like herding cats. Normally, royalties flow to the editor, although sometimes individual authors are paid for their contributions. In business, multiauthored works are usually articles and books written as part of the company's business activities. Engineers in a research lab might report on their work, a group of consultants on their methodology, a team of sales managers on how best to sell large capital goods, while another team might report on the results of a benchmarking project.

Group projects have been found to be excellent ways for companies to demonstrate their intellectual capital, garner prestige for the firm, and showcase individual employees. Increasingly in consulting, in particular, multiauthor books are appearing. These are considered major strategic marketing initiatives by their firm.

There is a huge problem here that you should be aware of: contributors come and go. In the first place, people are always flattered at being invited to participate in such a project and thus can be counted upon to say yes more often than no. Only the experienced author pauses and thinks about the commitment about to be made. Many people in business associate writing with their immediate job, so if they change positions (e.g., are promoted to a new job), they feel a compulsion to drop out—"let the next guy do it." Since most contributors have little or no experience today in writing, their ability to honor project deadlines or to deliver quality material is severely compromised. Grab a half-dozen professors to work on a project, and as a rule it goes through very smoothly. Grab a half-dozen business people, and you will limp across the delivery date finish line exhausted, frustrated, and with a few bridges burned behind you. It is the nature of the beast.

How can you minimize the problem? Several personal experiences with this exact problem suggest the following tactics:

- Try to recruit people who have done some writing, published or unpublished.
- Recruit people who could write someone else's chapter if that someone bails out on you.
- Use a ghost writer or communications person to rewrite sections of the text to make it seamless and cohesive.
- Tell all contributors that this assignment, if they agree to do it, transcends their job and that if they change positions, they are still expected to do the work.
- When creating the initial list of contributors, develop a backup list of at least one individual for each contributor; you will have to go to that list before the end of the project.
- Assume the project will take between 20 and 30 percent longer than normally would be the case with a single author, and make sure your delivery date in a contract with a publisher reflects that assumption.

These suggestions sound like the advice from a cynic, discouraging at best. Collaborative projects are wonderful experiences. When well done, they produce very high quality material, so they are worth undertaking.

Are there any other configurations of authors? The other most widely deployed arrangement is a combination of academic and company authors on a project. These projects have their pluses and minuses, too. On the upside, the project can tap into a variety of experts, giving the project additional credibility because it includes both academics and practitioners—a wonderful combination for a serious business book. Practitioners are more likely to reach out to academics than are professors to partner with practitioners. So, don't expect a call from a Harvard don, but you should not hesitate to invite an academic to play on your publishing team. On the downside, company lawyers want to impose constraints on the project, and those restrictions drive the academics nuts and cause some publishers to avoid getting involved in the project. The fight is normally over who owns the copyright, who gets the royalties, how much sensitive company material is being used, and what the professors might do with that data outside the confines of the book. Freedom of expression and opinions expressed are, surprisingly, less of an issue, although there probably is no professor alive who wants a manager or lawyer "editing" his material! Articles tend not to be a problem because the scope is narrow and controlled.

Involving academics is important as a strategy for gaining access to some journals. Some editors will almost insist on academic involvement so that the practitioner author will have a document that is packaged the way the journal wants. Such involvement has long been a strategy, for example, that enables practitioners to get published in such prestigious journals as the *Harvard Business Review* and the *Sloan Management Review*. Editors of academic journals will always deny that this strategy works on them because they like to think that they select material based on quality and relevance of content. But don't believe it!

A variation is to hook up a new or inexperienced author with an experienced one as coauthors. It is a wonderful way to mentor a rookie. You only have to do this once or twice before the rookie author has figured out what to do and can solo on her own on future projects. Some companies have actually turned this mentoring strategy into a formal process because it ensures people will write and produce publishable material that conforms to corporate guidelines. Reward your coaches and they will recruit more writers. It is a great strategy for jump-starting publishing in your firm.

Mentoring a New Author

The focus of this chapter has been on many legalistic issues, with a dash of lessons learned from the perspective of project management. But mentoring fits here because, in many companies, publishing occurs when someone within the firm with publishing experience is willing to help others write and publish. It is rare. On the other hand, firms that want to publish intellectual capital look around their pool of employees; if they find employees with experience, companies find ways to weave it into their publishing and knowledge management strategies.

Mentoring typically develops in one of two ways: by accident or by design. As publishing becomes increasingly popular in businesses, those who have quietly been writing over the years are asked by others interested in publishing to answer questions, even to critique manuscripts, and are recruited to help place items with editors. Those firms that want to use mentoring as a process, however, approach the issue very differently.

The first step is to designate an individual in the corporation with responsibility for promoting publications by employees. The second step is to identify who in the firm already is publishing and is willing to help others, then to put in place whatever incentives are necessary to encourage the experienced to assist others. The incentives could range from setting aside time from their own work to help others, time to write more, travel budget to go to different parts of the organization to meet with would-be authors. That person could also run writing and publishing seminars within the firm. Then, management should reward, celebrate, and recognize the efforts.

What does a mentor do? The challenge for a mentor is to expose a would-be author to the tasks of writing and publishing while simultaneously passing on necessary skills and sustaining the neophyte's enthusiasm for the work until it is published. Most would-be authors know something—they are experts on a subject—but know little or nothing about writing. Sending them off to an English class at the local community college is not practical. You will have to help them start putting words on paper, showing them how to organize their thinking, maybe even coauthoring pieces with them so they see the process at work. They have to go through this drill about three times before they know enough to dispense with a mentor. Using a ghost writer can be very helpful. The mission is to teach skills and to further tacit knowledge, not to transfer facts.

Would-be writers all seem to ask the same questions—the issues the book you are reading is about—and therefore the mentor fields many telephone calls, spends countless hours in staff meetings and "over lunch" gatherings, answering and promoting and encouraging people to try writing. To a large extent, mentors are cheerleaders urging people to write and then bursting with pride when their protégées publish. As momentum builds, that is, as people hear about the existence of someone in the firm who is willing to mentor, many will come forward. The problem for the mentor is which people to invest in. Many want to publish, few actually do. As a mentor, you will simply have to practice a sort of literary triage to determine who to invest in. As in medical triage, you separate people into categories: those who are wasting your time, those who might get some work done, and those who have the potential and determination to publish. You will spend time with all three groups, but you want to focus more on the third because those people become the basis for an expanded pool of mentors in later years. In a business environment, there is also a fourth pool that cannot be ignored, those whom you must help for political reasons. These could include your manager, who sees a way to publish by riding on the shoulders of a writing employee, those whom you are ordered to get into print, and so forth. That fourth group is usually small; you can handle them deftly by just writing a piece and listing the person as coauthor. Or, simply throw a ghost writer at the project and manage that effort as any other business initiative.

Mentors should, however, bring potential authors into research and writing projects when the other parties have something to contribute, such as expert knowledge. It is a wonderful way to write oneself and train others without skipping a beat. Mentors are in a better position, for example, to conceive of a major project—a book-length collection of chapters by multiple authors—as a vehicle for training a half-dozen or more people at the same time. Mentors themselves should continue writing and publishing, sharing their experiences while doing this, so others can see by example. Knowing and watching an author is inspirational because observing takes much of the mystery out of writing and publishing. Lifting the veil of the unknown, exposing the mystery of writing, may be the single most important act of a mentor. Once people know what the mentor knows, many will conclude that they, too, can write and publish, that they, too, have something at least as important to say as that individual.

At the nuts-and-bolts level, mentors often tell people exactly what to do, read and correct their various drafts, may call editors to place material or coach authors on how to do that, then celebrate these accomplishments. Mentors will get telephone calls on Saturday afternoon, will have to set aside time on Sunday afternoons and while on airplane rides to read manuscripts, and have to tell people very diplomatically how to improve their literary babies. Most of the material will be of very poor quality, often not suitable for publication. The mentor's challenge is to deliver that message without discouraging the would-be writer or to show an individual how to invigorate the material to make it publishable. To get closer to the latter positions, mentors should focus on several kinds of tasks:

- Force would-be authors to outline and to understand what the key messages are and for what audience

- Force would-be authors to write and polish, write and polish, then polish, polish, and polish

- Force would-be authors to show their material to other experts, then fix and polish

Don't let would-be authors treat the material as if it were an extension of themselves. Be cold-blooded about the content and quality of the material from the first contact. Would-be authors need to have the detachment of a third party, like a forensic pathologist doing an autopsy on their creation. The mentor must teach them this task.

As the process of mentoring develops, it will become clear who is going to write and publish and who is simply talking a good game. Winners are those who have something to write about *and* invest the time to put their thoughts on paper. Spend a great deal of time with those people because they will deliver results. I define results in this case as publications sitting on my bookshelf. Read their papers, really work them over to show how they can be improved and polished. Personally introduce your winners to editors, engaging them in the process of selling their material to a publisher. Once they have had a taste of success, push them to do more. *More* in this case means additional articles, sometimes with multiple writing projects going on simultaneously, and then, ultimately, a book. Set expectations for additional performance from your stars and cheer them on, reinforcing their confidence. These activities are very much what a good professor in graduate school does with a star pupil writing a doctoral dissertation. You see the same kind of behavior in a skilled craftsman teaching an apprentice, a carpenter bringing a would-be colleague along. It is showing, correcting, congratulating, and doing more of the same, and forcing a protégé to do as the mentor does until the skill is mastered. Mentoring frequently involves a multiyear relationship with an individual, cutting across jobs and career changes. There is no other way—it just takes time to train new writers and to get them published.

Momentum creates its own opportunities. For example, editors constantly solicit experienced authors to write articles and books. Somehow, good writers wind up in the Rolodex files of many editors, including in those of journals and publishers they have never worked with before! If busy, the good author normally declines the invitation. A busy mentor might say to the editor, "I don't have the time," or "I am not as qualified to do this work you want," but then adds the phrase, "but I know someone who is qualified and does have the time. And I'll work with her to make sure the manuscript meets with your satisfaction." Then, you talk the would-be author into taking on the assignment, with you as mentor to make sure it gets done right.

Over time, your relations with authors change. As they gain confidence, experience, and enjoy publishing successes, they will need less nuts-and-bolts help than before. Like peers, they will seek out your advice on messages and content and less on writing and publishing. It is then that you have to teach them to mentor others in the firm, bringing those others along the way you did them. Otherwise, your phonemail will remain clogged with messages from wanna-be's. It is in your self-interest as a mentor to expand the pool of like-minded mentors. This is particularly true in very large corporations, such as at my IBM, where a lot of really skilled people with lots of energy and ambition want help getting published. The same circumstance exists at such other firms as Philips, Citicorp, AT&T, General Motors, Mobil Oil, and so many others. In the companies just mentioned, employees have not hesitated to call me for mentoring. So, if the word gets out, a good mentor may be asked to help others in other companies! Recruit additional mentors!

A Case Study: A Factory Unto Himself

 James Martin is one of the most prolific authors in American business history. In 1996, he published his 100th book, *Cybercorp*. All his books have been on business topics, in fact, all on various aspects of information processing. Some have been technical books for IT professionals, others for business management, and some for folks like you and me.

James Martin began writing books on computing while an employee at IBM in the 1960s. His early books on database management and telecommunications became instant classics. He later published books on programming methodologies and application development. The company supported his work and eventually, after nearly two decades at the firm, he went out on his own. He continued to write books and eventually started his own consulting firm. Life has been good for James Martin.

But what made him a successful author that his publisher, IBM when he was there, and now the man himself can take pride in, was his burning desire to write and publish. He proved willing to do it within the realities of working within a corporation, in terms that made sense to the reading professional, and later in support of his consulting practice. The moral of his experience is that authors can be highly successful both out on their own or as part of a corporate structure. Employers, an industry, and publishers can all benefit from having a James Martin working with them.

In the United States, the First Amendment of the U.S. Constitution guarantees citizens freedom of speech against political suppression. Lawyers will tell you that First Amendment issues are between citizens and their government. Authors, however, feel it is always an issue between them and anybody who might want to constrain their expression—governments, religions, or corporations—and thus sometimes are at odds with their employers, talking at one level while the lawyers are on a different point. Authors have a tradition of cherishing the First Amendment, and so it becomes the source of contention when some organization attempts to constrain (authors say, censor) their ability to express themselves. The problem is not absent from the business environment.

The Key Issues:

- Ability to express one's opinions on any issue without fear of censorship or recrimination by the organization one works for
- Ability to write and speak on any topic

When This Right Creates Tensions:

- The firm might be harmed by revelation of sensitive or competitive information.
- The firm feels it must control what its employees say and write outside the firm.
- The firm is in danger of being exposed to criminal or civil suits or to competitive attack.
- The firm attempts to retain possession of its intellectual capital.

How Firms and Authors Deal with the Issues:

- The firm defines clearly what its publishing policies are and gains commitment of employees to adhere to them.
- The author uses common sense, understanding that it is not always in everyone's interests to give away intellectual capital, embarrass the firm, or reinforce competition.
- Authors and companies discuss potential publications, coming to an understanding on a case-by-case basis on what and how things should be published.

SUMMARY

The key message is to sort out the various needs and best interests of multiple parties, including the company, the author, and the publisher. Copyright and royalties are the two most debated issues, but the strategic value of publications for a company is rapidly becoming the most pervasive topic. Beyond these turf issues are some general rules of the road that cover most situations fairly well.

Don't:

+ Publish any company confidential material
+ Publish anything that would embarrass your company
+ Publish information directly of advantage to a competitor
+ Publish anything you are not sure is right to publish

Do:

+ Seek advice of subject matter experts and people in authority (e.g., management, legal)
+ Seek advice from publishers
+ Publish things that help the company's business interests

These rules of the road are few but powerful. You and your company have spent a great deal of time, money, and effort over the years developing intellectual capital that has economic power. All companies are built on information and skills. Part of exercising those in economically profitable ways is to discuss them in print and in other media. Not to publish can be as harmful as publishing the wrong things. Writing has its own intrinsic benefits—such as organizing in one's mind thoughts on a topic, thus making one a more productive employee—while leading customers to see authors as experts in subjects in which the company wants to excel.

As managers come to realize the value of publications and implementation of various knowledge management strategies, the strains discussed in this chapter will decline. In fact, they are already abating, beginning with consulting firms but also now extending to companies that provide extensive services. What new practices are coming into being is the subject of the future chapters.

But before turning to those, we still have some basic blocking and tackling issues yet to resolve. Publishing an article, monograph, or book is only half the job. Now you want people to get copies, read them, and be influenced by your wisdom. Most authors think that their work is done once the publication is out and on their shelf. Most companies make the awful mistake of simply either saying, "Gee, that's nice that you published" or totally ignoring what just happened. In short, most authors and companies do not take advantage of the hard work of publishing. How to really gain advantages from publishing is the subject of the next chapter. What has to be done is easy, fun to do, and very powerful. Let's see what has to happen.

7

What You Do After Publication

I feel like the dog that chased cars and finally caught one:
now what do I do?

– Unknown Canine-American

To really get the most out of a publication—article or book—requires that the author and her company work together to promote and distribute this material. This chapter will show you what to do, how, and why. It ends with a summary of best practices.

Once you as the author or as the company publish something, there is after-publication work that needs to be done to exploit all the efforts so far. In fact, some authors will argue that researching and publishing is less than 50 percent of the job; that is certainly the case with articles and frequently with books. You want to do more than just let the publisher distribute the magazine or book. Leave nothing to accident. You and your company have business to realize as a result of the publication. As an author, you might have the opportunity for lucrative speaking engagements, and there is always the requirement to help sell the "product" and yourself. The firm should also share your publications with other employees so that they can know what you teach in print. It also allows them to leverage their association with you in their own work.

This chapter describes how experienced authors and companies exploit publications. Many authors and companies fail to realize that many activities should be engaged in after publication. Too many leave it to the publisher to promote and distribute, thinking that magic will occur, Pulitzer Prizes will be handed out, books made into movies, and consulting firms named Number One that year. That does not happen unless you decide you want this to occur and make it happen yourself.

In addition to firms ignoring how to exploit publications, authors in a business setting do not have the time to "push" their publications. Some also feel awkward doing it. Both they and fellow employees may view these activities as self-serving. The firm should recognize that the problem potentially exists and step in to take the initiative in both encouraging and supplementing promotion of material. Since most companies do not have focal points for such activities, they usually have nobody at the switch to jumpstart and help. That situation, however, changes completely when a company takes seriously the need to publish intellectual capital or to promote use of knowledge management principles of operation. Then you see the good marketing habits that are normally applied in promoting products and services swing into action to help an author and publications.

How Your Book Gets Sold

But first, a quick lesson about how books are sold because, more than articles, books require extra effort on your part. Once the book is manufactured, publishers sell books in essentially four ways:

- Persuade bookstores to stock them on their shelves (usually for trade books)
- Advertise books in catalogs that go out to predefined audiences (usually to specialists)
- Telemarket specific books to specific audiences by telephone calls
- Ensure that virtual bookstores on the Net offer it for sale

In addition, publishers will send copies out to journals and newspapers for a book review, which further publicizes your book.

Actually, there is also a fifth way to sell books: bulk sales to corporations. For example, your company buys a thousand copies because you—a member of the firm—wrote the book. Bulk acquisitions are made by companies to hand out to employees and clients and to use in teaching seminars. Consulting firms do this all the time. Nothing helps a small consulting firm so much as a good book. In the 1980s, Brian Joiner launched a highly successful consulting firm, using as his spearhead the *Team Handbook*, a book he self-published and sold hundreds of thousands of copies. In fact, bulk buys from companies often are big enough for a publisher to break even or to make a profit before selling even one copy of the book to the public!

The company you work for often also markets business books. Such a firm might sell the book to participants in a training seminar—a very popular approach—or, as Tom Peters has clearly demonstrated, at speaking engagements at which a local bookstore turns up with boxes of your book and sets up a card table in the lobby. Sales of this type, although they may only amount to dozens at one speaking engagement, may lead to many others since business managers have a track record of buying multiple copies of a volume they read and liked. A sale of one copy can lead to subsequent sales of hundreds, if not thousands, of copies. You just don't know when that will happen. Companies also will call attention to a book through notices in internal newsletters and in correspondence, flyers, and publications aimed at its customers.

Yet companies often fail to promote the books of their employees, a lost opportunity to demonstrate core competencies and to deliver their message (i.e., thought leadership) to the market. The companies that know how to properly promote a book work with the publisher to get the author out on speaking engagements; they persuade newspapers to write articles and conduct interviews; and they distribute copies of the book to those employees who call on customers. If there is no coordination, then an employee who publishes a book must rely on the ability of a publisher to market. The biggest problem with this approach is that a publisher puts out many new books, hoping that some accidentally take off and do well. A company, however, since it only has to worry about one or just two to five books, can devote more attention to promotion. Furthermore, since companies are interested in pushing books as a lead generator for business, they are more concerned about exposure and prestige than in generating profits from the sale of publications; thus, they are not constrained in their marketing expense as is a publisher who must operate within a narrow bandwidth of profit and cost.

Another problem is that if the firm does not market a book in conjunction with a publisher, then it is up to the author to do so. Some authors are very good at this, most are not. Part of the problem is how much time authors have to promote their books if they are full-time employees. A larger issue is knowing what to do.

YOUR ROLE AS A PUBLISHED AUTHOR

As an author, however, you do have a responsibility to help market your book. Experienced authors know that this means selective involvement in the selling process. Table 7.1 lists the major activities.

Your first involvement should begin at the time you write the book, to determine who the audience should be for this volume and to ensure you have defined a large-enough community of potential readers/buyers to justify the book. These clusters of potential readers can come from mailing lists that you can buy; your publisher can help you identify which ones and how to get them. They can come from your own company's pool of customers or from membership lists of professional associations. Begin by determining what category of professionals you want to target (e.g., lawyers, engineers, marketing executives, CIOs), then find lists of these people to validate the number involved. Let your company do this if at all possible because someone else in the firm typically has access to the material and has the infrastructure and resources to work with it. Sometimes publishers will prepare advertising brochures and flyers that can be mailed out to thousands of potential readers. Your firm should be able to help with this task as well. If the publisher writes the copy (text) for these flyers, make sure you read it, just as you should read the copy proposed for a dust jacket, to make sure it delivers the right message and properly identifies who you are. Yes, sometimes they even misspell your name!

Table 7.1

Major Activities in Marketing a Book
Telling the publisher which publications should review your book
Participating in radio, TV, newspaper, and magazine interviews
Going on book tours hosted by the publisher (rarely done unless you have a "hot" book)
Making presentations where you can promote the book
Notifying the publisher of where you will be speaking so they can arrange to have books sold there
Persuading your company, if it is supporting your effort, to hire a publicist to help market the book
Having your company, if it is supporting your book, buy copies in bulk, distribute it to employees and customers, and exhibit it at trade shows

Table 7.2

Sample Questions Publishers Ask of Authors
What are the five key selling points of your book?
Who is the key audience for your book?
Do you intend to promote your book on a personal Web site or by other electronic means?
Do you give any seminars?
Would you be willing to make author appearances?

Your second point of involvement occurs at the time the manuscript is put into production—after it has been accepted for publication—when the publisher will ask you a series of questions on a questionnaire that relate to marketing. Table 7.2 is a typical example of the kinds of questions asked, in this case, the ones presented to me for this book. It is very important to take the time to answer the questions carefully because you may know more than the publisher about who should buy the book, which journals should review it, and where advertisements and events would yield results. To illustrate the effort, Table 7.3 shows the answers I provided for the book you are now reading.

Your third involvement comes at the time the book is physically published and is now in a warehouse, ready to be shipped to cus-

Table 7.3

Sample Questions Answered for This Book

What are the five key selling points of this book?

1. It is practical, based on my personal experience over 25 years.

2. It is also based on the needs displayed by over 200 people I have mentored in business publishing.

3. It is clearly written and to the point.

4. I have implemented both the writing and program development suggestions and they work.

5. There is no other source on the topic; this is it.

Who is the key audience for this book?

This book has two audiences: those in business who want to publish regardless of rank or industry, and those who want to run a corporate-sponsored publishing program. Logical groups include consultants, training personnel, communications experts, engineers, and middle to senior managers. Those whose profession is the use of knowledge and expertise are particularly important audiences for this book.

Do you intend to promote this book on a Web site or by any other electronic means?

Yes. I will post announcements on my company's internal Web sites and electronic bulletin boards, link it to a Web site a colleague and I have, and link to other logically appropriate Web sites. I will put sample text on-line to illustrate the content and style of the book, particularly the Table of Contents and parts of the preface.

Do you give any seminars?

I routinely teach seminars within my company on publishing. Once this book is published, I will do three things: (1) increase the number of seminars I teach internally, since I will have a teaching aid—the book—to help me; (2) offer a similar seminar outside the firm as a way to generate additional revenue for my employer; (3) lecture on the themes of the book at conferences (e.g., why publish).

Would you be willing to make author appearances?

Yes, I would: interviews by radio, TV and the press, book signings, presentations at conferences, even presentations at companies willing to buy many copies of the book, willing to consult on how to estalish a corporate publishing program. I would welcome PTR's help in placing me as a speaker in various conferences, such as for trainers and communications and PR.

tomers and bookstores. A number of activities occur at this time. Experienced authors have already had prior conversations with their companies in the three to four months prior to physical manufacture of the book to hammer out what the firm will do to promote the book. But once the book is published, there are many things that an author can do. For example:

- Indicate to the publisher other places to send the book (e.g., specific radio programs, industry newsletters).
- Speak at conferences where the publisher can have copies of the book for sale.
- Discuss with individuals the contents of the book—a great source of sales!!!
- Make yourself available for newspaper, radio, and TV interviews.
- Offer to appear at bookstores to promote, autograph, and speak about the book.
- Publish articles on topics related to the book (remember to write these months in advance for a journal issue that appears *after* publication of your book).
- Make sure that you, your firm, or the publisher puts notices of the book out on the Internet.
- Do the same for internal company publications (e.g., electronic bulletin boards, newsletters).
- Identify who might buy bulk copies within your company and line up those sales, or point the publisher in the direction of specific people.
- Put your publisher and industry trade associations together to discuss joint marketing and use of your book (also a great idea to pursue at the time a publisher is considering accepting your book for publication).

The list could go on, but these are the few and most effective steps you and your company can take. For most books, the amount of time required by an author to be an effective promoter might only be a couple of hours per month for several months. If the volume is a best seller, or your employer really wants to push the book, then it can be a full-time job. But normally, the effort is less than that.

An author also has to take the lead on foreign translations. Most publishers do a terrible job in trying to negotiate foreign translations because they get such a small percentage of the royalties on foreign imprints. The big publishers have either foreign subsidiaries (e.g., Oxford University Press) or links to foreign publishers (e.g., McGraw-Hill), while all have contacts. Properly placed in key foreign markets, your book can generate as much interest as in your home market. Key markets for business books include all English-speaking countries, Germany, France, Japan, Korea, Latin America and Spain, Brazil, and to a lesser extent, Portugal, and Italy. Everyone else either represents too small a market to justify a translation or the people who would care about your book read one of the major languages, often English. If you used a literary agent, you should know that the best ones are good at lining these up soon after your English edition goes into production.

One gesture that translation presses like to use is a newly written preface prepared for their edition by you. Simply write a new preface targeted at the audience the publisher is going after, and, as part of that publisher's job, the firm will translate the new preface along with the book into the local language. That is the easy part; the hard part is getting them to give you copies of the translated book when it comes out; they often forget to send you these!

The last step you should take to support the book is to discuss follow-on books with the publisher. This is more than a "son of" strategy, it is how the next book can help sell the last one. Michael Porter has written several books on competition, and in each one he reminded his readers of the previous ones and how one built on the other. James Martin, who writes on information technology, has taken this strategy to an art form because for many years his books were, in effect, part of a large series all written by him! If you, as a reader, find useful a second or third volume by an author, you are inclined to go back and hunt up the first or second publication and read that too. This happens with business books as much as it does with novelists like Steven King and Tom

Clancy. So, you want to make sure your earlier books are available in the market when your next book comes out. That is your responsibility, particularly if your second or third book is published by a publisher different from the one who did the earlier book; the first publisher may not know you have another coming out unless you tell him so. In the final analysis, you are the logical integrator. So, how do you do that? Telephone the marketing department and tell them what and when you are publishing, and work out with them what will be done. It is as simple as that.

Maximizing Sales and Leveraging the Book or Article

Are there some actions that can be taken to maximize the impact of an article or book? The answer depends on what your objective is.

If your objective is to get your message out as part of a company-supported program, you would do the following:

- Distribute, free of charge, books and reprints of articles to current or potential customers through your existing marketing channels (e.g., sales representatives)
- Put copies of articles and unpublished white papers on the Internet
- Personally distribute reprints of articles
- Attempt to place articles in foreign language magazines and journals
- Distribute widely among employees single or bulk copies of articles and books

If your objective is to sell copies of a book, the activities with the most impact are:

- Selling copies at conferences at which you speak
- Doing interviews on television, followed by radio, and always industry-specific print media

- Running seminars for a fee on the subject of your book and distributing the book as a benefit of attending the course
- Offering to sell multiple copies of books at bulk rates at seminars and conferences
- Distributing your book jointly with industry or professional associations
- Getting into the "right" book catalogs

Authors and publishers often overlook the last point. For example, if you write a book on quality management practices, you want to make sure that the ASQ Quality Press carries it in their catalog where they also offer books by many other publishers—that list goes out to people who really are interested in quality management publications. For a training book, get into ASTD's catalog. There are many regional bookstores that do a terrific job in target marketing catalogs. My favorite is Harry Schwartz Bookstore in Milwaukee, Wisconsin, which puts out one of the best business book catalogs in the United States. It goes out to thousands of business people who buy books. Don't know what catalogs exist? Begin by paying attention to the ones you receive now. Next, discuss the issue with your publisher; they know who to go after.

Articles can be used in some ways more conveniently than books. For example, they can be included in proposals to customers to demonstrate that you and your firm have skills in certain areas. Some companies, particularly consulting practices, may bundle up several of these into what amounts to a fancy scrapbook of reprinted articles to demonstrate their skills. Kuzmarski & Associates, an outstanding U.S. consulting firm specializing in brand management and product marketing, does this about as well as anyone in the world. For them, it is an advertising tool as well as a way to celebrate the work of individuals within the firm.

Both books and articles can be packaged or reprinted as part of a companywide marketing program to increase visibility with constituencies who are not customers. For example, as industry associations do all the time, send these publications to individuals who influence the fate of your company, such as government regulators, state and national legislators, key industry influencers (e.g., associations and industry commentators), and academics who research, write, and speak on your topics. If you care about a particular company's or individual's opinion of your ideas or your firm, put them on the mailing list for copies of your stuff. Remember the obvious: those people only read what they have. If they have your material instead of someone else's, then you know what they might read.

This last suggestion can have serendipitous effects. A personal story illustrates this. Back in the mid-1980s, I sent several books I had written to a Pulitzer Prize-winning business professor; he was grateful. Over the next several years, in his own work, he began to cite my publications. Then in the early 1990s, he agreed to be quoted on the dust jacket of one of my books, saying what a terrific book it was, breaking his own rule of not providing testimonials of this type! The negotiations for the testimonial went on behind my back between him and the publisher, and I only found out about this wonderful event two weeks before the book came out. The moral of the story is that your mother was right: you should be nice to everyone! It really is a small world.

One final suggestion, rarely used, but sometimes possible, is republication of articles and white papers in anthologies. Other magazines and books for republication sometimes pick up particularly outstanding articles. For example, McGraw-Hill's *Quality Yearbook* reprints articles and book chapters that the editors consider to be outstanding. Some article authors have figured out that this is another channel of distribution and don't hesitate to try to convince the editors to reprint their material. Another reprint strategy is to collect a group of articles on a related theme by one or more authors and interest either a book publisher or a company in republishing them. The Harvard Business School Press does this routinely with collections of articles that originally appeared in the *Harvard Business Review* and that are all related to a topic (e.g., information technology, leadership).

Anthologizing material like this is actually a good service to provide because it saves readers the time and effort it would take to hunt down key pieces. Given the enormous explosion in the amount of material available today on any topic, it has been increasingly useful to turn to publications that have selected the best to present. In fact, there are whole magazines and journals that do just that, and others do the same thing selectively (e.g., an Oldie Goldie article originally published 25 or 50 years ago that is now considered a classic). Books on business and technical milestones are sometimes also reprinted on the occasion of an anniversary. Publishers like MIT Press, Springer-Verlag, and the IEEE have routinely done this for decades with technical publications.

Reprinting material is an expanding trend. In addition to the examples above are ones mentioned earlier: placing material on the Internet and repackaging whole chapters into new books and electronic publications. Thanks to computers, reassembling material has become quite simple to do, and given the ease with which paper-based publications can be manufactured quickly and cheaply, one could expect to see more of this kind of activity. Companies and authors normally do not take the initiative to explore these options, but publishers do. Given what authors know about the market, it would make sense for them to get really good at this. At a minimum, these alternative publications increase exposure and even other opportunities to generate more royalties.

ONGOING WORK WITH YOUR BOOK

University presses will keep your book in inventory and thus available to the public for years. Commercial publishers will sell the bulk of your book in the first year, will invest almost no marketing or advertising in the second year, and in the third year will probably dispose of almost all the remaining inventory to wholesalers and discount book distributors. Warehousing is expensive, and publishers are reluctant to continue investing in advertising. After the first year, they assume whoever should have heard of the book will have, so why promote? Exceptions are the best seller that usually lasts a little longer on the market and the perennial classic that may sell a certain number each year for many years. But normally, a business book has a shelf life of less than three years. As an author or a member of the firm that employs the author, you have a question to answer: for how long do you want to push the book?

If the volume is a relatively popular one and has predictable and consistent demand, you may want to take the steps outlined throughout this chapter and continue them for multiple years. Textbooks and technical reference material fall into this category because they do not get outdated as fast as most business books. One common strategy is to publish second, then third and fourth editions. A new edition is normally a revised version of the original book in which you have done one or more of the following:

- Added new material
- Updated existing material
- Corrected errors
- Did a combination of all three
- Made the book longer

You might have dressed it up differently, too, with sidebars and more illustrations in the second or third editions. Some books that are periodically revised become classics and stay in print for decades. Professors are excellent at this, we in business are only just learning how to implement this strategy. Peter F. Drucker's classic, *Management*, was originally published in the early 1970s and now, in the late 1990s, it is still available and has been printed in various hardback and paper editions, along with many of his other books. Tom Peters now boxes some of his books together into sets. He also has made videos of the topics of his books, and these can be bought as part of a book package or independently.

Particularly well-known authors are increasingly bringing out portions or all of their books on tape that one can listen to while driving to work. Stephen R. Covey, for example, has various collections of tapes that repeat the themes in his books. Tapes cause sales of specific books to continue long after they normally would die on the vine. So here we are, nearly a decade after Covey published *The 7 Habits of Highly Effective People,* still selling thousands of copies each year!

Similar strategies have also worked for other books. Remember *The One Minute Manager*? In fact, that became a series, just like the Dummies books for computers. If you have a PC and buy the Dummies book for Windows or OS/2, you then are more likely to go back and pick the one published on your word processing software or about your spreadsheet package.

But why keep bringing out revised editions? There are two reasons: subsequent successful editions make more money than earlier ones and they build market awareness of your ideas. Revised editions have a stamp of prior approval for your work and owners of the first edition will often acquire the second if it is a significant improvement and expansion over the earlier one. Multiple revised editions means you have more copies of your book in more hands than before, in effect, acquiring intellectual mind share for your ideas. Prentice Hall's tax guides have guided the thinking of a generation of accountants; Paul Samuelson's sophomore college economics textbook represents the sole knowledge about the subject for tens of millions of Americans; industry directories and guides often serve as the only source on your industry. It is a way to come close to cornering the market on mind share for a topic. I am better known for publishing *The Quality Yearbook* than for some of my IT management books, even though I would prefer to be known for my work on information technology. Why? Each year, sales of the *Yearbook* keep growing, copies of earlier ones probably circulate around various offices, and my name keeps being put in front of people, especially subscribers of the book, year in and year out.

If you were clever enough to write a book such that the subject would not become dated, you can nurse sales for years. What is a book that becomes dated? Examples include

◆ Writing on the software problems associated with the Year 2000—guess when that book will be done with!

◆ Publishing a guide to filing your 1996 U.S. tax forms

◆ Producing a book on this year's Baldrige criteria

- Writing the best of 1997 in the world of Quality
- Elucidating the Clinton Administration's Reinventing Government strategy

On the other hand, these are O.K. to do if you and the publisher understand that the life cycle of these books is less than a year. Yearbooks are the classic example, but these are designed for a short sell-cycle, and subsequent editions normally are constantly under development.

Since business and technical publications today are as much victims and beneficiaries of fashion, of what is "hot" today, as is any novel, authors and publishers do not have as much control over circumstances as they would like. However, the more that you can infuse your book with timeless quality, the better the chance that it will remain relevant to buy and read three, five, ten, and even twenty years from now. Whereas books describing the functional characteristics of a 1998-era PC will not be attractive in 2009 when everyone will have forgotten what a PC of the mid-1990s looked like, a book on the principles of supply chain management may remain relevant.

Even highly technical themes can age well. For example, Frederick P. Brooks, Jr., wrote a book called *The Mythical Man-Month: Essays on Software Engineering*. He published this thin volume in 1972, based on his work as the project manager for the IBM System/360 and its operating system (OS/360), both developed in the 1960s. The book was still in print a quarter century later, had become "must" reading for software project managers, and was celebrated as a classic.

Another way to keep your ideas alive is to rewrite the book, using similar themes and messages, only repackaged. James Martin has done this frequently. Another example: Paul A. Strassmann. In 1985 he published an important book, called *Information Payoff*, on the transformation of work and the role of technology in influencing it. The book was well received and sold many copies, but eventually, Free Press, which published it, stopped selling it. In 1990, Strassmann published a second book, *The Business Value of Computers*, that incorporated many of his original ideas from 1985 along with much new material. Some readers of the second volume then went back to secondhand bookstores looking for the 1985 publication.

Authors reading this chapter may be thinking, "I can write articles and books, but I don't think I can do all these things suggested here." They may very well be right. Time is always a chronic problem. Some of these activities are expensive, and an author may not be willing or able to invest in the project. But more frequently, the real problem is that promoting a book calls for a different set of skills than writing it. In fact, "writer promotion" is almost an oxymoron. The introspection required of an author hardly seems like the entrepreneurially driven activities of a publicist or marketeer. The best practice is for the firm to promote publications and to keep the author producing more of them. Often, when a firm decides to start supporting publications, they make a critical mistake: they put their author in charge of the company's promotional activities. The qualities that made the author good are not necessarily the characteristics of a good PR person. After a while, the firm realizes this and turns responsibility for promotion to someone experienced in these matters. Most authors will accept the assignment in the belief that this will give them more time to promote their own publications and to write others. Nothing could be further from the truth. Now they are forced into mentoring roles, market development, and other communications functions that take them increasingly away from creating knowledge, which was the thing that originally caught everyone's attention.

 As the author you are in the best position, however, to take the lead on certain activities. First, you should pay attention to changes in the subject of your writing to know when your book is no longer current. When that happens, talk to your publishers about the pros and cons of writing a new edition. If the earlier one did well, the editor will want to pursue a revised edition. On the other hand, if it did not but you feel the topic's "time has come," go to another publisher. You may have to get permission from the first publisher to produce a second edition (depending on the terms of your original publishing contract), but it is always worth a conversation. Most book contracts have a clause that gives the publisher the right to request a revised edition. You may or may not be in the mood to write a new edition, so the subject is always open to debate. Where publishers take a hard line is with annuals and reference books, which they can get someone else to update and which normally have predictable sales. In these situations, you have to understand that you will be requested to update frequently. With normal trade books, that circumstance is rare. In most instances, it makes more sense to write an entirely new book, with fresh material, like Paul Strassmann did. If the subject has moved far beyond your original edition, then an entirely new book is in order.

SUMMARY

There are essentially four activities related to publishing that are always evident whenever you encounter an effective author or a company deeply involved in exploiting its intellectual capital.

First, *researching, writing, publishing, and promoting are all parts of a never-ending continuum.* The job is never done when the book is just written or published. To a lesser extent, the same holds true for articles and videos.

Second, *pursuit of a subject, conducting research, and applying insights are the central activities.* Publications should be treated as spinoffs of the central task of discovery and use of information. Too many people do the reverse by saying they want to publish an article or book, when in fact, they need to be discovering and applying knowledge.

Third, *multiple types of publications should emerge from research and use of information.* Part of getting the word out may involve narrowly focused, issue-based articles, a book from time to time, and other electronic communications. The point is: you will not be effective in communicating to the public through one medium or infrequently; you must use numerous articles and other forms of publications to get the job done.

You have heard the old phrase "Heaven helps those who help themselves." Promoting an article or book calls for the same virtue. Aesop, the ancient Greek story teller, spun a tale about Hercules and the wagoner that makes the same point.

One day, a wagoner was driving a heavily loaded wagon down a muddy road, when the wheels on his wagon sank deep into the road. The horses couldn't pull the wagon forward, so the wagoner, frustrated and irritated, called on Hercules to help. The god appeared and said to him, "Lean on the wagon, wagoner, encourage your horses to pull, and then you can call on me for help. If you don't help yourself, why should I or anyone else assist you?" The man did as he was told, followed through, and Hercules helped.

The issue is one of taking responsibility and following through. Let's listen to Aesop make the point that there is no reward without hard work. Remember the story about the farmer and his sons? The old man was about to die and so he called his sons to his bedside and told them he had buried a great treasure out in the vineyard. He said, "Dig for it and you will find the treasure." When the old farmer died, the sons went out into the field and dug, and dug, and dug everywhere out there looking for the treasure. They never found it, however; but as a result of turning over the soil so often, they produced a magnificent crop of grapes that they presumably converted into marketable wine.

An American author, Ralph Waldo Emerson, understood:

> Brave men who work while others sleep,
> Who dare while others fly—
> They build a nation's pillars deep
> And lift them to the sky.

Fourth, *more publishable topics arise than there is time to write about*. Therefore, focus on what is important to you and your company. Write the articles and books that will most support your personal and business objectives. In other words, learn to say no to projects that are not germane to your interests and expertise. Publishing for the sake of publishing does not do much for you or the firm.

Speaking of "the firm," authors in business do not operate in isolation. They function best when their work environment nurtures research and writing. Using intellectual capital to gain competitive advantages, to grow market share and revenues, and to apply knowledge to improve efficient operations is no accident. It is always the result of a well-crafted corporate strategy to exploit intellectual capital. How that is done is the subject of the next chapter.

8

Running a Corporate Publishing Program

There are no secrets to success. It is the result of preparation, hard work, and learning from failure.

– General Colin L. Powell

This chapter focuses on what companies should do to support individual employees conducting research and publishing. It reviews proven strategies for providing support and infrastructure, discusses how to focus on what is important to the organization as a whole, and illustrates examples of tasks that can be done. Finally, this chapter discusses how to develop measures of success and improvements.

More and more, organizations are coming to the realization that managing their intellectual capital is crucial to their success. This intellectual capital affects everything from how to improve core processes to how to speed up the design and delivery of new products to market, from concept to cash. Those things do not happen by accident, hence the reason for a tremendous effort underway today by companies to become "learning organizations." If you were looking for the next area of focus following reengineering, it probably would be the management of learning and of intellectual capital. But having intellectual capital is useless unless employees can get their hands on it, use it, and add to it.

143

Part of that process of handling information involves publishing. What an organization needs to do to facilitate that effort is the subject of this chapter.

WHY TO DO IT AND WHAT IT IS

 If you do not have a way to disseminate intellectual capital, you might as well not have any because it can't be used. Shared intellectual capital comes in two forms:

- Data available within the firm for the exclusive use of employees
- Information made public for use by employees, customers, and others

The first form is typically the source of much activity today, where companies build intellectual capital systems by using such tools as Lotus Notes, the Internet, and other technologies to capture information and make it available on-line to those who need it. Consultants build intellectual capital with their methodologies and consulting tools; product designers build by storing templates for components and gizmos; process owners collect information on the performance of their processes. However, discussion of these systems lies outside the scope of this book. For our purposes, it is enough to know that these systems need to be in place because these pools of information, that is, data within our area of interest, can be the source of potential articles, books, videos, and CDs.

Go to any medium-sized or large company and you will find two facts to be true: somebody is doing some publishing, and people will complain that they have no time to do it. Engineers, sales representatives, consultants, trainers, middle managers, doctors, plant managers, PR people, and researchers will tell you the same thing. What does get published may or may not be consistent with what the corporation is doing as a whole. For example, if an information technology or telephone company wants everyone to know that the future of computing is linked tightly to networks, then having an employee of that firm publish a wonderful article on the physical characteristics of the next generation of computer chips, while very interesting to other engineers, does not support the message this company wants to communicate. On the other hand, if that author had written an article on the role of computer chips in the construction of future telecommunication networks, now there is a match between what the corporation wants to discuss and what the individual is doing.

If a company decides, therefore, that employees should publish, then it is appropriate to apply resources of the firm to channel the writing energy in directions that benefit the corporation as a whole. Publications are, to put it bluntly, another form of advertisement, although on a far more sophisticated level. It is an alternative form of indirect marketing because publications establish credibility, announce that your firm is in some form in the business that the publication is about, and attract leads to the company and potential partners (for joint marketing, product development, etc.). Therefore, the first decision a company must make is whether there is value in encouraging employees to publish. If the answer is no, you have finished reading this book. If the answer is yes, then read on!

Before you dismiss publishing as a concerted effort, you should realize that in today's marketplace your competitors are not only competing for sales of their products but are also waging a war to gain mind share. Advertising has historically been the primary tool to get the job done. However, given the growing addition of services to products, where personal and institutional credibility is as important as any widget you might sell, publications become a way of winning the war on mind share. In the early 1990s, one major consulting firm ran an advertisement for many months that listed how many of their employees had Ph.D.s and M.B.A.s, and how many books and articles these people had published, all in a column ending with the statement that this firm brought a lot of know-how to the table. It was a powerful example of taking writing to the next step in the war for mind share, using advertising.

Companies that encourage their employees to publish usually also pay attention to what their competitors are doing. The battle of the page ends up being another variation of publish or perish, a war fought on business battlefields, not left to professors fighting for tenure. Companies will even go further and attempt to dominate or influence channels of thought leadership, such as prestigious academic journals or through carefully orchestrated networking with key editors of newspapers, magazines, and TV and radio programs. These techniques are so common today, particularly in North America, that companies can no longer assume their competitors are not practicing them, regardless of the industry they are in!

Basic Activities

Once a company's senior management accepts the need to encourage and support publication, even before anyone can develop a strategy for getting the job done, management must begin by understanding what employees think about why publication is not happening today. Typically, you will hear five reasons for lack of activity:

1. It was never considered important.
2. Don't have time, work 55 hours a week already on regular work activities.
3. Company does not reward thought leadership expressed in publications.
4. People do not know how to write and publish.
5. Access to training about the management and use of intellectual capital does not exist.

However, the biggest issue will be that employees do not believe they have enough time to publish, given their already heavy workload. Many would like to, lack confidence in how to go about it, or are nervous about doing something wrong.

Understanding current employee issues is only a first step. Next, the company needs to decide what areas of intellectual capital it wants to major in. If you are a consulting firm specializing in change management and have a great deal of engagement experience and intellectual capital, it probably makes sense to publish on the subject. If your product design department has an excellent reputation for high quality and innovative work, you may want employees to demonstrate those commitments through publications concerning design and innovation (e.g., case studies). If your company believes it has some core competencies, you may want to accent those. Some examples:

- ◆ Xerox is very good at benchmarking, so its people have published articles and books on the subject.
- ◆ AT&T Universal Card is good on call centers and customer service, so their people have published on this subject.
- ◆ IBM is confident that it understands the evolution of computer technology, so guess what a lot of its engineers publish on? They even have their own highly respected journal (*IBM Systems Journal*).
- ◆ Just about every consulting firm picks its specialties and publishes on these topics.

How to communicate your message is always a question of strategy. Normally, these strategies have four components to them:

- ◆ Research projects done internally or with partners (e.g., university professors) to create intellectual capital
- ◆ Publishing programs to get articles and books out on what you know
- ◆ Networking to exploit existing publishing relationships, to be quoted in the press (in preference to somebody else), and links to speaking opportunities
- ◆ Conferences, with programs to sponsor, host, or participate in because these provide opportunities to get the firm's message out

The good end up doing something in each area, the best coordinate activities across all four. The best will also tell you that this is not a short-term program but rather a multiyear strategy.

Table 8.1 catalogs how long key activities must be done before a company realizes measurable positive results. As you can see, this is not a quarter-by-quarter business!

Table 8.1

Long-Term Strategies for Recognition		
Activity	How Long It Takes	Comments
Research and writing of books	2-5 years	Even an exisiting manuscript takes six months to publish.
Research and writing of articles	Weeks to months	You may have to wait a year or two before an editor can publish it.
Recognition as The expert (the one called by *The Wall Street Journal*)	1-5 years	Personal and institutional, social, and professional networking required.
Membership on editorial boards, boards of directors of organizations	3-10 years	Prerequisites are expert status, public track record, professional networking.
Speaking engagements and conference host	1-2 years	Once started, these gain momentum and gain a distinct advantage

A related set of tasks involve overcoming obstacles faced by employees in researching and publishing. Let's take the list from above as an example.

1. *It was never considered important.*

Maybe it never was. If it is important to publish now, then you must understand why and explain that conclusion to employees, telling them how publishing fits into the overall strategy of the company. You can do that through executive presentations, changes in job descriptions, in seminars and other training interventions, allowing people to join organizations and to subscribe to key publications at the company's expense, and by rewarding those who do. *But the key is to tell employees that writing for publication is important, that you want them to do it, and that they will be supported and rewarded for their efforts.*

2. *Don't have time.*

There are many ways that companies deal with this issue. Technical writers often are asked to write during regular office hours as part of their job. Others are given time off to work on publications, much like a mini-sabbatical for days, weeks, or months, staying on the payroll but just not doing their regular work. Fellowship programs are common among many high-tech companies. Bell Labs has many employees who work full time doing research and publishing; IBM gives its brightest researchers time to pursue their ideas and to write. Some consulting firms give utilization credit to their employees for writing; others provide support services to reduce the amount of time required for publication, such as providing ghost writers and PR people to find publishers.

3. *Companies do not reward thought leadership expressed in publications.*

Once companies declare that something is important, they should reward behavior in support of that. A number of steps can be taken, such as:

- Paying for research materials (e.g., subscriptions, trips to seminars and conferences)
- Giving time off to do the work
- Awarding cash and momentos for a job well done
- Promoting and giving salary increases to exemplary performers and role models
- Publicizing an individual's work in company speeches and internal publications
- Distributing copies of publications to colleagues
- Writing executive thank-you letters

4. *People do not know how to write and publish.*

Don't just give them a copy of this book. Most people do not know what the writing and publishing process is, have no contacts in the publishing world, and would not know how to begin if they had to. A common way to fix this problem is to have the communications arm of your business reach out to potential authors and work with them

- to mentor
- to teach the subject in seminars
- to connect authors and editors

Some firms will actually create organizational infrastructures to support and teach authors, the subject of the next several pages.

5. *Access to training about the management and use of intellectual capital does not exist.*

The problem normally is very basic: management may not have yet figured out what intellectual capital is and its value in the marketplace. Once that hurdle is overcome, then comes the obvious one about how the company should promote and sustain publishing efforts. The first problem is fairly easy to solve because business management literature today is full of suggestions, best practices, and case studies on the subject. Some of the best of that material is cited in the back of this book. It speaks to the core activities of the organization. With regard to promoting publications, by comparison there is little in print. Yet a number of steps can be taken to address the problem:

- Ask the communications departments of other companies what they do.
- Call authors in other firms to find out what is done and how they are supported.
- Conduct formal benchmarks with other companies.
- Seek information from acquisition editors of publishers who regularly work with companies.

This last suggestion is often a very effective first start. Begin by looking at recent publications to get a sense of who is publishing and call the publisher to speak to an acquisition editor. Book publishers are better than magazine or journal publishers on this score. Some of the most knowledgeable, because they publish multiple publications from the same firms, include Prentice Hall, McGraw-Hill, John Wiley, and Oxford University Press, to mention a few obvious ones. But talk to the business acquisition editors, not those who work with history, cookbooks, and so forth. Questions they can answer are summarized in Table 8.2.

Table 8.2

Questions to Ask an Acquisition Editor
What kinds of business publications do you handle? Who else in the publishing firm handles them?
Do you, or your firm, have experience dealing with multiple publications from one organization? If yes, tell me what that relationship is.
Who has the responsibility for creating and adopting manuscripts for the series? How is that done?
How do you and my company handle marketing responsibilities? In detail, please!
How do you both treat royalties?
What do you consider to be the best way for a company to support its own publishing program?
How would a publisher be interested in partnering with a firm?
What would make it a "win-win" for both companies?

If the acquisition editor is not interested, ask with whom you might talk in other publishing companies. You should be prepared to suggest what a series from your firm might be about, how many books per year you want to publish, and how many copies your company might buy per year. These are issues the editor will want to discuss with you in order to answer your questions.

The information you gather will then enable you to figure out where in your organization to house the initiative required to pull together a plan to encourage publications. Small companies usually assign the responsibility to one person, e.g., in marketing, public relations, or communications. Larger firms may have several pockets of support and design. For example, the research arm of a company may have a communications department that can provide support; the consulting arm of the business, a marketing consultant-type; a corporate lawyer who worries about copyrights working with an outside PR firm. The point is, there are many variations; the best have at least one person who worries about building the strategy and implementing programs in support of publishing. Often, several people from across multiple departments will work together to launch the process. Later, a formal organization can be put in place when the work is constant and of sufficient quantity and value to warrant staff.

There is always the danger of putting carts before horses, however. To avoid that, you should realize publishing programs are the backend or end product of something more important, like research. The best managers see publications as an expansion of the research activities of the firm. To do otherwise would mean simply cherry-picking what is already available for publication without any organized means to replenish intellectual capital. Without a constant supply of new ideas and case studies, you would run out of things to write about that are important enough to support the strategies of the firm.

Tapping into all departments and divisions of a company is also important because they represent both a larger pool of material to exploit and can lead to better-quality, higher-value publications. Thus, for example, having an engineering department and a brand manager working together could lead to a robust publication on innovation in product development. Another cogent example is an accountant and a consultant discussing the value of ABC accounting in support of process-managed marketing.

Linking research, publications, presentations at conferences and seminars, and participation in national associations leads to new research and publishing opportunities, improves the skills of employees, and opens access to publishing outlets. In short, these steps increase your chances of gaining the high ground in a mind-share war.

To jump-start the process, if you have not already done so, immediately assign someone the responsibility of worrying about the subject and of putting together the strategy for implementation. The first cut on a useful strategy should take only a week or two to do. The strategist needs to know, however, that the publishing initiative will take several years to get into high gear and thus should act accordingly. That means, for instance, not expecting people to drop what they are doing and rush to their word processors and not anticipating that editors will immediately publish what is produced. Appointing a person does, nonetheless, take you from the intangible "I wish my folks would publish more" to "Here is what we got done this year," because eventually momentum kicks in and things do appear in print and circulate among those whom your firm wishes to influence. Dedicating such a resource is the fastest way to go, even more so than hiring a public relations firm—the PR folks don't necessarily know your company or its intellectual capital, nor do they necessarily have solid credentials with book publishers, serious business journals, or conferences. Save the PR resources for such things as advertising and working with business trade magazines, or writing press releases and speeches for executives.

ORGANIZING AND DEPLOYING FOR RESULTS

The keys are commitment, deployment, and infrastructure. To a large extent, we have already discussed commitment; you have to decide that publishing is going to be supported. Addressing the five major concerns of employees begins to demonstrate commitment. Accepting that this commitment must run for many years is another aspect of the issue. Now, you must deploy resources to meet the commitment.

We have already discussed the first resource: one or more person to build the support and to facilitate getting the job done. Creating another department is not the answer; you need a knowledgeable employee who can mentor, find publishers, get people networked, and form virtual teams to drive specific projects. The normal role for such an individual should include:

- ◆ Promoting publication of articles, books, videos, etc., relevant to the business

- ◆ Fostering more research and thought leadership focused on the company's core interests

- Providing publishing access to employees and teaching them to develop their own accesses

- Identifying alternative ways to showcase company thought leadership by means of other resources within the firm (e.g., advertising, communications, marketing)

- Serving as a role model, personally doing some research, writing, mentoring, and speaking

Ideally, your publisher leader/coordinator/guru should have intellectual capital recognized as valuable both within and outside the company. That person should already have experience working with editors and publishers; there's no time for another employee to acquire those skills—it takes years—and you must hit the bricks running.

Give your leader a rank that middle managers will salute; it is from the middle tier that your individual will have to recruit support for your publishing goals. A lieutenant would have a difficult time recruiting a colonel! So, should this person be a second- or third-line manager? An executive? A senior consultant? It depends on what you think would work in your company. You might ask, What should the job title be? A universal title does not seem to be emerging, so invent one that make sense for your firm.

Whatever the title, your publishing leader should report to someone very high in the organization in order to cross divisional and departmental boundaries and to be freed from cultural and political problems. In short, your publications person needs a well-placed political godfather, like a senior vice president.

If research is not well organized in your firm, then you face the problem of addressing that issue before publishing. An increasingly popular model is the use of competencies. Figure 8.1 illustrates an example of such a network of competencies.

Members of a competency do the following:

- Conduct research

- Collect intellectual capital from daily work and company projects

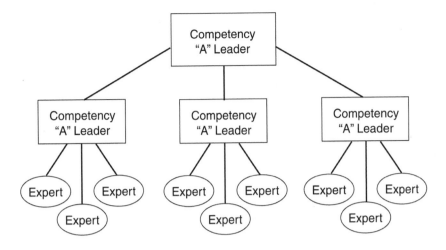

Duties

- Research
- Teach
- Participate/perform
- Speak
- Publish
- Share with other competencies

Results

- Growth in intellectual capital (IC)
- Expanded use of IC across the company
- More effective performance
- Wide public recognition
  of your company's skills

Figure 8.1   Competency Network

- ◆ Store and make accessible this intellectual capital, usually in computer systems and company libraries

- ◆ Conduct research projects with professors and customers

- ◆ Teach and mentor other experts in these areas

- ◆ Participate in conferences in their subjects

- ◆ Publish case studies, methodologies, results of surveys, and major research projects

Competency leaders tend to report to vice presidents of research and often are populated with competency experts recruited by leaders from across divisions, disciplines, and departments as a virtual team. They routinely meet to share information by telephone, groupware, or in person. Competencies can be the source of a great number of publications because here are the experts, and after a while, they recognize that they are the experts!

Armed with one focal point and a collection of competencies, you can now move from commitment and deployment to create an infrastructure that facilitates execution, which in turn leads to results. Generally, employees need eleven types of support:

1. Seminars on how to write and publish articles and a different seminar on books
2. Someone within the firm or hired by the company to clean up their text or ghost write books, produce films and videos
3. Already established links to "favored" publishers for those writing books
4. For articles, someone who has contacts in the publishing industry (e.g., a communications agent)
5. Someone who can arrange for them to speak at conferences
6. Budget for seminars, conferences, subscriptions, and travel
7. Access to internal publications, e.g., newsletters, electronic bulletin boards, monographs
8. Company guidelines on policies concerning copyrights, royalties, "do's and don't's"
9. Mentors for those new to publishing
10. Management insistence on paying attention to and measuring results
11. Graphics and word processing support

As the publishing process matures in a company, several patterns of behavior become evident. For one thing, you begin to see the company publishing in ways that are attractive both to employees and to customers. For example, you see the Big Six consulting firms publishing monographs or highly prized management journals. For another thing, you see established events become recognized for providing value. For example, IBM and Clemson University have jointly hosted annual conferences on process reengineering, change management, and customer rela-

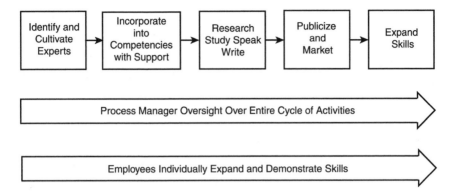

Figure 8.2 Evolutionary Steps to Leadership

tions. For a third, you see experts routinely called upon to comment on national events and on specific topics. We see retired military officers working for Washington, D.C., think tanks providing commentary on television on national military crises (e.g., Persian Gulf War). Another: stock brokers are constantly quoted in newspapers, magazines, and on television about trends and events involving specific companies and industries.

None of those things happens by accident. As Figure 8.2 suggests, they evolve into activities through a process that leads from expert status to publication and speaking and thus to demonstrated knowledge and thought leadership. Eventually, people come to those individuals—and to their companies—for information, assessments, and advice.

Some firms create databases of experts that can be tapped by newspapers and electronic media for fast access to experts. A few consulting firms now even have hot lines that one can call, for a fee, for quick answers on such issues as tax law and government regulations.

Other firms have targeted key publications and electronic media for special handling. In this situation, a company will assign someone to be a point of contact for an editor, to provide that publisher with such services as writers for articles, access to quotable experts, support for initiatives of a magazine (e.g., conferences or awards programs), and referees for articles and books. Because such corporate contacts are often at the cutting edge of newsworthy issues, editors listen to them.

The question of promoting a book always comes up. If your company is supporting the book, then it should, as part of getting the word out, promote the publication. In addition to the various ideas described in this and earlier chapters, you can take another step: hire a publicist. A publicist can promote the book by getting newspapers to write articles about it, can place your author on radio and TV programs, etc. Normally, you hire publicists by the project and pay them by the hour. Once your firm has several books (e.g., three to five) it is promoting, then it may become cost effective to hire a publicist as a full-time employee. But why a publicist? As I stated earlier, publishers do not spend enough time on one business book to make it a winner, so you have to do it. However, as many seasoned publishers will tell you, any book can be made into a best seller if you invest enough time and effort into promoting it. By the way, a "best seller" status can be achieved for a business book—along with all the publicity that goes with it—just by selling only 40,000 to 50,000 copies; you don't have to sell a million, although that is nice but rare with serious nonfiction.

Measuring Success

By this stage, companies are also measuring results. Table 8.3 is a collection of sample measures that can be used by a company just starting to promote publications and access to the press. These measures focus on activities because everything begins with action. The key in the early stages is activity, not results; those will come later. Focus attention less on the cost of these activities. The most expensive part is advertising and that is already being measured by someone else in your firm.

Table 8.4 has a more subtle set of measures designed to indicate the effects of publishing. You want to move from the first to the second, but it takes time, often years.

Other collateral measures related to the management of intellectual capital are often in evidence. These can include number of patents (all high-tech companies keep score), percent of revenues

Table 8.3

Sample Measures for a Company Just Starting to Promote Its Expertise

Experts and Competencies
- Number of experts identified who potentially should speak and publish
- Percent with previous publishing experience
- Percent that wrote this quarter, this year
- Percent of experts now members of key associations or academic alliances

Volumes of Publications
- Number of white papers written this quarter, this year
- Number of articles written this quarter, this year
- Number of articles accepted for publication this quarter, this year
- Number of books and videos produced this quarter, this year

Speaking
- Number of speaking engagements this quarter, this year
- Number lined up for next year
- Number of individuals speaking this quarter, this year
- Percent of speeches converted to white papers or articles, this year

Quotations and Citations
- Number of times an employee was quoted in the press, on radio or television, year-to-date
- Number of articles published on your firm or the subject of radio or TV spots

Advertising and Marketing
- Number of publishing alliances established by type (magazines, book publishers, etc.)
- Number of editorial board memberships this year
- Number of targeted magazines/journals in which your firm advertised
- Percent of targeted magazines/journals assigned a contact from your firm

Table 8.4

Sample Measures for a Company Highly Experienced in Promoting Its Expertise

Experts and Competencies
- ◆ Same measures as in Table 8.3
- ◆ Customer data on perception of company's skills, by country or market segment
- ◆ Percent growth in number of experts by skill level
- ◆ Percent of experts in leadership roles in key societies and industry associations
- ◆ Number recruited to support a government or industry project or who testified before national legislatures or government commissions

Volumes of Publications
- ◆ Same measures as in Table 8.3
- ◆ Number of articles and books actually published, translated
- ◆ Number of book reviews appearing in targeted journals
- ◆ Number of articles appearing in targeted Tier One* publications
- ◆ Need: A set of measures on partnership performance with publishers

Speaking
- ◆ Same measures as in Table 8.3
- ◆ Percent of speakers rated Poor to Outstanding at conferences and compared to other speakers
- ◆ Number of attendees at conferences cosponsored or organized by your firm, trended over time
- ◆ Number of speakers covered by the press
- ◆ Percent of speakers who have published a book or a video
- ◆ Number now charging for speaking engagements, number of events

Quotations and Citations
- ◆ Same measures as in Table 8.3
- ◆ Number of quotes and citations in Tier One* publications

Advertising and Marketing
- ◆ Same measures as in Table 8.3
- ◆ Output of publishing alliances
- ◆ Public feedback on expert image of company

*Tier One = those half-dozen journals in which you must appear. This list can be by industry, profession, country, or continent. For example, if you are touting expertise in finance and accounting, your employees must publish in *CFO*; if in quality management practices, in *Quality Progress*; if in general business management, *Harvard Business Review*.

generated from products less than 4 years old (e.g., 3M does this), number of competencies, and the revenue they generate in consulting (e.g., IBM). There is growing evidence that leading Japanese companies have altered their job descriptions and corporate culture to foster general knowledge growth throughout the enterprise. In the back of this book, I include material on this fascinating subject; the bottom line is, Japanese companies take it seriously. The research communities in most companies also have a broad range of measures of expense, revenue, new inventions, efficiencies, effectiveness, customer receptivity, and so forth, that often are also looked at. The key to measurements is to clock what is important, producing the few and the mighty metrics and related information relevant to your business but always covering the entire spectrum of concerns:

- creation of intellectual capital
- its improvement
- its publication
- its effect on your customers and on your bottom line

Figure 8.3 is a high-level value chain suggesting the scope to which measurements must evolve. In the final analysis, senior management will want to know how a publication strategy is working. There are two reasons for this concern:

1. Publishing programs grow more expensive over time—a cost in employee time and in collateral budgets for writing travel, research, and publishing.

2. Published messages can have a positive or negative effect on markets and customer perceptions of the firm.

If your organization is increasingly using a balanced score card approach to measurements—a strategy I personally endorse—then Figure 8.4 suggests what some measures might be for publications in an organization that is already well down the road. As the creators of the balanced score card, Robert S. Kaplan and David P. Norton would argue that there is no fixed set of perfect measures, merely those that make sense because they provide a

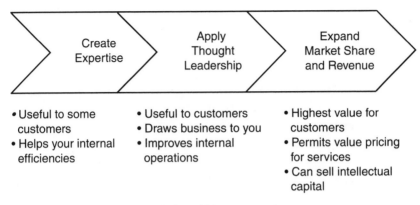

Create Expertise

- Useful to some customers
- Helps your internal efficiencies

Apply Thought Leadership

- Useful to customers
- Draws business to you
- Improves internal operations

Expand Market Share and Revenue

- Highest value for customers
- Permits value pricing for services
- Can sell intellectual capital

Evolution of Measurements

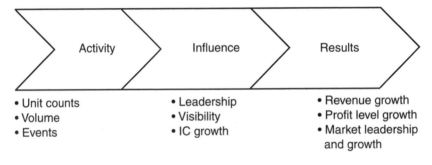

Activity

- Unit counts
- Volume
- Events

Influence

- Leadership
- Visibility
- IC growth

Results

- Revenue growth
- Profit level growth
- Market leadership and growth

Figure 8.3 Measurements Value Chain

broad view of reality. Their advice is very appropriate for this chapter.

Finally, we have the basic question to answer about costs for such programs. There are no hard rules of thumb to follow. However, we know the categories of expenses an individual or firm can have. Using these categories of expenses, you can calculate what they might be for your company. Some of the obvious categories are the following expenses:

For the individual:

◆ Subscriptions to one to five journals and magazines

◆ Purchase price of 5 to 20 books per year

◆ One week's worth of travel to a conference and the expense of the conference

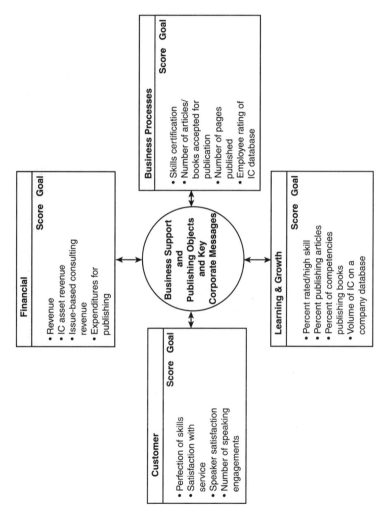

Financial

      Score Goal

- Revenue
- IC asset revenue
- Issue-based consulting revenue
- Expenditures for publishing

Business Processes

      Score Goal

- Skills certification
- Number of articles/books accepted for publication
- Number of pages published
- Employee rating of IC database

Business Support and Publishing Objects and Key Corporate Messages

Customer

      Score Goal

- Perfection of skills
- Satisfaction with service
- Speaker satisfaction
- Number of speaking engagements

Learning & Growth

      Score Goal

- Percent rated/high skill
- Percent publishing articles
- Percent of competencies publishing books
- Volume of IC on a company database

Figure 8.4 Sample Metrics Scorecard

- Graphics and typing unless you already have that capability in the firm
- Dues to one to four organizations
- Rewards for a job well done (whatever amount your company normally uses)

For infrastructure:
- An individual's salary and benefits for fostering publishing
- Ghost writing expenses (e.g., $10/page)
- Acquisition of copies of publications for distribution
- Extensive travel to institutions, conferences, and employees (e.g., 20-30 weeks)
- Corporatewide memberships (3-5)
- Conference support and hosting (can range from five thousand to hundreds of thousands of dollars)
- Postage, terminals, Internet access fees

For corporations as a whole:
- High-tech firms spend between 2 and 5 percent on research and development; to get going, plan about 1/10th of 1 percent for publishing initiatives if a major corporation; otherwise, something under $100,000 unless you are publishing a journal.
- Journals that you publish can cost you between $200,000 and $1 million plus, but you can eventually also make a profit on the journal.
- Cost of competencies, depending on the number of people, could range from tens of thousands of dollars to millions (see for the individual, above, for base costs).
- Publishing expenses for small monographs and brochures (thousands to tens of thousands of dollars for each, depending on quantity and length of publications).

These are generalized categories of expenses. If you are attempting to do this in multiple countries, costs for travel, employees, and translators, go up. Many of these expenses probably are occurring in the firm already. The key point to make about expenses is that they can be almost nothing or run into the millions. You can expect, however, that they will rise as (a) you put emphasis on publications and (b) you identify measurable returns on that expenditure. The intellectual capital can be treated as an investment that generates reusable revenue-generating material; everything else falls into the category of operating expenses. Both types of costs can be expanded or reduced very quickly. However, the return is greatest if you commit to a multi-year set of investments and operating budgets.

A Monastery Shows the Way

High in the Pyrenees Mountains overlooking Barcelona, Spain, is the ancient Benedictine monastery of Montserrat, fabled in history as the storage place for the Holy Grail. Monks carved their monastery out of the mountain in about A.D. 700. Napoleon tried to burn it down when his French armies invaded Spain at the end of the eighteenth century. The monastery sheltered individuals critical of the long reign of General Francisco Franco from the 1930s to the mid-1970s. For over a thousand years this monastery was the cultural headquarters of the local Catalan culture. During the same millenium, it developed one of the largest libraries on religious subjects on Earth. It has fragments of the New Testament, Greek manuscripts, and books by every major Western thinker since civilization began.

Montserrat has served many purposes for the Church and its Spanish community, and one very important function has been to conduct scholarship on religious issues. When a pope had a question that needed research, quite often he turned to the Abbot of Montserrat for help. The monks are scholar-priests, most speak many languages, and have advanced degrees from universities from around the world. Put in business terms, they have a great deal of intellectual capital, core competencies, and a well-defined market that they serve. The monks of Montserrat have been publishing for centuries. It is a core mission of this Benedictine monastery. If anyone has figured out best practices for an organization that must support itself and sustain itself against wars, plagues, and bad weather, it is this monastery!

Their strategy is simple to describe. They recruit highly educated monks who have important skills in the areas of research, writing, theology, and related humanistic subjects. They invest in a library that has everything from Greek manuscripts to Internet access. They have a librarian who tends to the collection and continuously acquires new additions. They have a publishing arm that physically produces books, pamphlets, and a journal for monks. They have had this publishing arm for a very long time. Thus, any monk who wishes to do research has a library available in the building; he has colleagues who can stimulate his thinking, critique his research and writing, and others to acquire materials, publish, and then distribute them. The monks publish constantly; they answer research questions from Rome; they help craft issues for the Catholic Church of Spain. In short, they are thought leaders.

They branched out to incorporate defense of the local culture of Catalonia many centuries ago and thus reached out to partners in the community. They publish histories of the region; their books are for sale in the bookstores of Barcelona, and the literary leadership of the region looks to Montserrat for help and support. The monastery is therefore a genuine source of regional pride, a "must visit" site for many Spaniards (particularly newlyweds, but that is another story), and has produced many highly placed church leaders. This is an organization that knows how to survive, thrive, endure, and take the high ground on issues of importance to its mission and long-term objectives. Yet it delivers results in the short term, quarter-by-quarter, century after century.

Summary

The key messages in this chapter are the following ones:

- You must create an infrastructure that will encourage and support employees in their efforts to publish.
- You must clear out the cultural underbrush that inhibits creation and dissemination of intellectual capital by eliminating constrictive guidelines while rewarding positive publishing behavior.
- You must have a companywide strategy and assign someone the responsibility for creating, running, and improving it.
- You must establish corporate links to sources of intellectual capital (e.g., customers, universities, other organizations, and people) and outlets for writing (e.g., journals, book publishers, and conference hosts).
- You must plan on this being a long-term initiative.

This last point may be the most difficult for management to accept, but it goes to the core of what is happening in commerce today. Industries are desegregating and forming new configurations driven by core competencies of potential partners, as a consequence of new information technologies to make those actions possible. Knowledge content is rising in products and services; decisions increasingly are being made on criteria beyond simple costs, increased speed, and reliability. Creative entrances and rapid departures out of markets are causing new business ecological environments to be built. Everything is driven by knowledge, with intellectual capital now rapidly becoming the gold in the treasury.

That gold is also the coin of the realm, and in this new world, publications take on an importance never before seen in business. Just as you would develop and implement strategies to design, build, sell, and support products and services, so too must the same be done for the new gold—intellectual capital—and that requires commitment, resources, and deployment. No longer can an individual employee here or there sporadically do research or publish; that employee is too valuable not to be aimed at a real business target.

How do knowledge management and publishing relate to each other? Are there synergies with both that can be exploited? The emerging subject of knowledge management is the subject of our next chapter. The two topics are intertwined more than most people realize. One is difficult to leverage without the other.

9

Knowledge Management and Publishing Programs— a Perfect Marriage

The great end of knowledge is not knowledge but action.

– Thomas Henry Huxley

T his chapter defines knowledge management, best practices emerging in that arena, and how publishing and knowledge management work together as part of a more comprehensive strategy.

Simply put, publishing is not only a way to share knowledge with others but also a method that forces one to catalog and organize some of a firm's information so that many people can use it in an intelligent fashion. Having files lying around in electronic databases or in file cabinets in paper folders is not knowledge management. To make knowledge management useful in helping a firm turn a profit, it must be accessible to many employees in a format usable by them. Furthermore, since we expect authors to understand what they write about, they become experts others turn to in a company for information. The experts have to organize their thinking and knowledge in ways that make it possible for them to apply this organization and to share insights with others. Since publishing accomplishes that goal, it becomes yet another set of disciplines for placing the right knowledge in the right parts of an organization. Publishing is a tool for leveraging and applying knowledge.

WHAT IS KNOWLEDGE MANAGEMENT?

Knowledge management comprises the various business tasks performed to collect, analyze, and disseminate information and insight. It is the act of methodically using the skills of groups of employees in ways that benefit an organization and cause useful insights, information, and skills to be transferred around the enterprise. Components of knowledge management include the collection and retrieval of information in computers, databases, and networks (usually called collection of facts, or explicit knowledge). Other sets of components are the practices of an enterprise that lead to the sharing of information stored in the heads of employees (usually called tacit knowledge, such as insight). These activities can include traditional training programs, departmental meetings, mentoring processes, developmental projects, use of teams, conferences, sharing rallies, and employee retreats. Knowledge management also is the organizational constructs that are established to facilitate the collection, cataloging, analysis, and distribution of knowledge management. These constructs can include the job of information czar, a department of knowledge management, intellectual capital support, and competencies of experts who use technology, meetings, and personal networks for the purpose of learning, applying, and sharing information.

The use of technology, corporate culture (including organizational constructs), and a growing body of business and managerial practices makes knowledge management come alive. Knowledge management is particularly relevant in business where experience, subtle insights, and less-than-clear information must be brought together to result in something. In the "old days," a craftsman acquired skills, information, insight, and improved all of these over time, learning to acquire explicit and tacit knowledge. He learned by doing and understanding and reflecting on his actions, often with an experienced mentor at his side.

What kind of knowledge needs to be collected, organized, and shared through the use of knowledge management techniques? Some examples suggest what is often involved.

- Training an airline reservations clerk to spot a potential terrorist who wants to buy a ticket
- Knowing when a customer might be ready to buy additional features and services with a car
- Understanding the profile of a successful criminal prosecution
- Knowing when to write an article that is a case study as opposed to a formal description of a process
- Appreciating the kinds of insights that a "hunch" provides
- Sensing when a car just does not sound right, even though you cannot explain that something is wrong

The question always remains, how do I take the experience of highly trained and knowledgeable people and pass it on to newer members of the firm? Expert systems (artificial intelligence at a primitive level) barely scratch the surface. You can't ask someone with thirty years of experience to tell you everything he knows; that would take thirty years to accomplish. Yet a lot of work has been done over the past half-century to understand how people learn, how institutions acquire and apply core competencies, and the act of intellectual sharing that is being applied to knowledge management. In fact, many of today's knowledge management experts know as much about human cognitive functions (a fancy way of saying how the brain works and learns) and about epistemology and pedagogy (how people are taught) as they do about corporate change management practices and information flows. The new element is the formal application of management practices of corporate change, cognitive sciences, and process management to create environments that leverage and grow knowledge institutionally. All are required to implement practical knowledge management.

In many organizations this is, initially to a large extent, the merger of man and machine, of databases and personal experience, of reliance on terminals attached to databases full of useful information and transference of experience from one head into others by means of mentoring. The challenge for management always centers on getting the most knowledge out of people and into an environment where it can be shared in a suitable manner with all other employees. Besides the obvious advantage of getting more people using good knowledge is the security that the firm's success will not depend on the experience of one or a few people. As corporations increasingly have to compete on knowledge and skilled services, the firm must increasingly acquire knowledge independent of any one individual. Downsizing taught management another lesson: that important corporate knowledge has legs and can walk out of the enterprise. The cost in some industries (e.g., high-tech) was far more than CFOs reflected in annual reports. The subject thus has acquired new features. Hence the raging interest in knowledge management today.

The tasks of knowledge management are best described in a formal way. The first step is to decide what kind of information and knowledge you need and why. Second, you put in place a process and technology for the routine, formal collection of this data. Third, the information is then cataloged and organized in a way useful to those who must rely upon it. Fourth, you have to create the infrastructures, culture, and incentives to ensure that employees are constantly updating and adding to this base of information. Fifth, converting information into knowledge through a variety of media now becomes essential (e.g., mechanically, it would be through mining data; humanly, through analyzing, drawing conclusions, and teaching best practices). Finally, you must apply knowledge in some way beneficial to the firm, e.g., in application of more effective sales techniques or getting to the source of an employee problem.

Providing post-activity assessments on what did and didn't work enhances the formal process. Some sales organizations debrief after major selling campaigns are over. The U.S. Army always debriefs after any field exercise. National political parties do post-mortems on won and lost elections. Debriefing leads to knowledge management if, at its end, the participants formulate a set of results and conclusions that later practitioners of the same activity can use to ensure equal or greater success.

Is anybody doing this debriefing? In fact, all groups of people practice knowledge management, if only because people are curious and introspective by nature. IBM salesmen learned as far back as the 1920s to debrief after sales calls. Managers hold annual retreats to look back on the past year and forward to the next. Yes, people practice knowledge management all the time. When corporations realized in the late 1980s and early 1990s that core competencies were crucial to their success, executives began to impose managerial discipline on the process. The experience of the 1990s strongly indicated that knowledge management definitely drove benefits to the bottom line, sometimes in a dramatic fashion and always in many innumerable ways. Insights and skills were recognized as competitive advantages, and paths of learning led to first entrant benefits (e.g., patents and higher market shares) while leaving competitors in a weakened or declining position within a market. Almost every major corporation in the world thinks it is now competing on competencies. Nearly the same number would argue that they are extensive users of knowledge management.

Although this is not the book in which to carry on a detailed discussion about how best to manage knowledge, it is worthwhile to note some rules of the road essential for anybody to understand in order to exploit the benefits of publishing. These are essential insights for appreciating how best to apply publishing to the broader objectives made possible by knowledge management. That is why best practices are essential elements of any publishing initiative. They cannot be initiated by the individual author; only management can implement the strategy across an entire firm because it takes many people working together to create and improve the kinds of bodies of knowledge that make for great publications.

BEST PRACTICES IN KNOWLEDGE MANAGEMENT

Although activities in the general subject area of knowledge management have been going on for many decades, only since the mid-1980s did managers consciously start thinking of the topic as a branch of management practices, and only since the mid-1990s as growing in importance. One byproduct of that new awareness is research on what are the best practices in knowledge management. To be sure, the subject is expanding, its practices are being tested and documented, and we have much yet to learn. But insights of sufficient quality are beginning to come in, so that one can plan with confidence how best to use them.

Larry Prusak, who wrote the foreword to this book, studied some 100 knowledge projects during the 1990s. In the process he learned why managers launch such projects. The reasons boiled down to three:

- To make knowledge and information both visible and available through a variety of tools, such as on-line yellow pages, applied hypertext, and knowledge maps

- To create a corporate culture that exploited knowledge through such behaviors as sharing of information and knowledge, and seeking and collecting additional useful insights

- To develop an infrastructure that supported knowledge, such as technical infrastructures, connections among employees, collaborations, and availability of a variety of tools and techniques

Prusak observed that the most effective managers paid close attention to the combination of human, organizational, technical, and strategic issues and factors that influenced how knowledge was used in an organization. Hoarding creates enormous problems; understanding why and how to use knowledge was of great value to the firm.

There is a huge debate underway among experts on the interrelationships of types of knowledge and their use. The experts are concerned about the role of context and dependencies. Some see communities of workers sharing knowledge as crucial and, therefore, want to understand how we can foster that behavior. Others think of knowledge as a product with markets within and outside of the firm, in which people acquire, use, dispense, and sell knowledge and insights. Whether the flow of knowledge is described as a pseudomarket or as communities of sharing, from a tactical perspective the issue boils down to making knowledge available across the enterprise in a timely and useful way. We will come back to the role of publishing as a vehicle for packaging and disseminating information and knowledge.

We are beginning to the catalog the types of knowledge activities that companies find useful. Rudy Ruggles, who has studied knowledge management in practice, identified eight types of activities (*Knowledge Management Tools,* 1997):

- Creating new knowledge
- Accessing useful knowledge from outside the firm
- Applying knowledge in decision-making
- Embedding knowledge in the activities and products of the firm
- Demonstrating and communicating knowledge in documents, electronic files, and software
- Encouraging collection and use of knowledge within a corporation by building a culture that values it
- Moving knowledge around the enterprise to make it useful to as many employees as possible
- Assessing its value with measures of knowledge assets and impact on management

Much of this activity begins with technological infrastructure and process management, but then people discover higher orders of use and recognize that knowledge applied to the firm's daily activities provides as much value as technological applications.

What inhibits or stops the use of knowledge management in firms today? The key surveys all tend to point out the same issues. The foremost issue continues to be corporate cultures that do not value knowledge or facilitate its use in daily activities. Not far behind is the failure of top management to give knowledge management importance, the same finding noted by many scholars in the 1980s and early 1990s with the failure/success of quality management practices—senior management failed to back the initiative. Third on most experts' lists is the lack of any shared appreciation or understanding of a business strategy that incorporates the use of these tools. Interestingly, most lists place in fourth or fifth place organization, yet organization invariably is one of the quickest ways by which management seeks to cause change. A CEO simply appoints a Chief Information Officer and says, "There, I have started the process." All the usual reasons of failure for any business initiative fall much lower in surveys (e.g., staff turnover, poor technical infrastructure, incentives).

Normally, listing best practices as a list of "don'ts" or negatives is not an effective way to communicate what to do that works. However, Liam Fahey and Larry Prusak teamed up to combine their research on best practices in knowledge management in the late 1990s to create a short list worth remembering. Viewed as a collection of errors, here is their list:

1. Not developing a working definition of knowledge
2. Emphasizing knowledge stock to the detriment of knowledge flow
3. Viewing knowledge as existing predominantly outside the heads of individuals
4. Not understanding that a fundamental intermediate purpose of managing knowledge is to create shared context
5. Paying little heed to the role and importance of tacit knowledge
6. Disentangling knowledge from its uses
7. Downplaying thinking and reasoning
8. Focusing on the past and the present and not the future
9. Failing to recognize the importance of experimentation
10. Substituting technological contact for human interface
11. Seeking to develop direct measures of knowledge

Fahey and Prusak's prescription for success reflects the findings of other researchers and practitioners. They argue for sharing an organization's knowledge with employees at multiple levels of the enterprise. However, their research strongly suggests that knowledge is always localized, e.g., in the heads of individuals or in small groups of employees often in close physical proximity to each other (e.g., in the same department or floor). They find the most useful applications of knowledge occur when employees are given many opportunities to discuss and debate the definition and use of knowledge, not just simply the business issues of the firm. Increasingly, they find employees need help to identify what should be, or are, their roles as creators and users of knowledge. Management also must ask employees to articulate the implications for the group's behavior and processes in applying knowledge. Just as process owners discovered with operational processes in industry in the 1980s and 1990s, knowledge management processes can be improved upon, both in content and application. The caution here is not to focus strictly on information or facts, but also on what people think they know as they make decisions on behalf of the firm.

The rationale for using knowledge management techniques is still being debated and is just now becoming a widely recognized "next step" for many management teams. The situation we find with knowledge management is not so dissimilar to that faced by managers in North America and in Western Europe in the mid-1980s with quality management practices, particularly process management. The parallels are remarkably similar, the prescriptions and best practices almost identical. That is good news—we can borrow from the best practices of the last major addition to management practices to implement knowledge management effectively and more rapidly. The critical task will be to develop a culture that values knowledge and a series of processes that create, share, and apply knowledge. What those processes are and how they work continue to remain a cathedral under construction. The experts know, however, that the processes include creation, movement, and leverage of knowledge, along with their organization into useful forms and their dissemination. It is in the last step that publishing can play a crucial—although not definitive—role.

Researchers are constantly refining their understanding of how best to apply knowledge management. Key research interests at the end of the 1990s centered around:

- ◆ Exchange of tacit knowledge
- ◆ Flow of information
- ◆ Making knowledge assets visible

But although one can make a short, general list, the tough questions don't lend themselves to cataloging. For example, much attention is being paid to the evolving role of knowledge in organizations, not just in business, but in all types of institutions. Other people are interested in identifying strategic-level barriers to the use of knowledge (where the debate arises about knowledge as a new form of capital or competitive advantage). An extensive debate is underway on what and how to measure knowledge. Then, there is the large issue of identifying operational barriers to the collection, organization, use, and improvement of knowledge. The intangible quality of knowledge and its anthropomorphic value (because it resides in our heads) lead many managers to struggle with a definition. But, it often is that lack of precision and its impalpability that gives knowledge a quality that makes it inaccessible to competitors. There is competitive advantage here!

Yet one's impulse is to the visible, to the tangible, to the accessible. Publications play a key role in these arenas. That is why there is a strong link between publishing and knowledge management, why we must understand their relationship. When well linked, the two support the business objectives of the enterprise.

LINKING KNOWLEDGE MANAGEMENT AND PUBLISHING

Knowledge management experts are co-opting language from many disciplines to help articulate their ideas. One useful concept borrowed from archeologists is the notion of an artifact. A knowledge artifact is a piece of knowledge, not a piece of data. We care because publications are more like artifacts than data. This book you are reading has some data (e.g., how many business books are published in the United States in one year), but more often, knowledge (e.g., how long people take to write a book and why). Data lacks that higher order of analysis. Now look at an archeological artifact—the shard—a broken piece of pottery. The scientist looking at that artifact can deduce from it many things, such as when a particular village used containers for food and water, the degree of artistic skills as evidenced by the art painted on the container's surface, maybe even something about the society's values derived from the themes and style of art on the object. In other words, a shard offers more than a specific piece of information.

Publications broadcast many messages at various levels to the reader, just as a shard does. The quality of the paper on which something is printed suggests a certain image that the publisher wishes to portray (e.g., quality, collectability, value, or throwaway). The layout of the material on a printed page suggests whether it is intended for a technical audience, whether it invites a reader to look at it, and how messages are to be communicated (e.g., combination of text, color or black-and-white illustrations, charts, and graphs). Publications serve as a form of intellectual and business branding by creating an impression in the mind of the reader even before the material is read. Thus, the author, like the pottery maker of old, communicates far more to the reader than words on a page or sound bites in a video. Because of that, publications are more closely aligned to knowledge management than to information or data management.

An artifact is also a thing, regardless of any messages it may deliver. One of the byproducts of knowledge management is insight or knowledge. They also are objects that contain knowledge. A key output (or deliverable) of knowledge activities normally is a file, paper, book, or video, in other words, a physical container of knowledge. Output is always an issue business managers worry about concerning knowledge. They want a tangible quality to it. That is why they often want to know what is being produced, besides smart people with a head full of good information. They look for knowledge artifacts as a surrogate measure of output. They also look at the results of more knowledgeable people—what the knowledge experts really want you to focus on—but still artifacts are indicators of positive or negative activities. Therefore, the production of various types of knowledge in the form of publications becomes a widely used option within knowledge management programs.

Quite often today, knowledge managers focus on just building technological infrastructures to stimulate dissemination of knowledge. Hence, the great interest in e-mail, Lotus Notes, competency databases, and so forth. But electronics by themselves are only conduits of information, even though they can stimulate knowledge-enhancing behavior on the part of employees, customers, markets, and companies. Another complementary source of knowledge, one that we touched on in Chapter 1, is the publication; it forces the author and the reader to combine information with other experiences, data, and insight to create what we call knowledge. Thus, as managers develop knowledge management strategies for a business, they have to consider the role of publications.

To that end, you can ask several questions of your knowledge management strategy.

- How can we use publications to deliver messages to our employees?

- How is that cheaper, better, or more effective than through electronic means (e.g., Intranet sites)?

- How can we use publications to deliver messages to our customers and suppliers?

- How is that cheaper, better, or more effective than through electronic means?

- When is a publication a more practical tool than a verbal or electronic message?

- What are the advantages of paper vs. electronic messages?

- What kind of publication is most effective and easiest to get into the hands of our audience?

- To what extent can our internal or external audience handle a publication?

This last question relates to access to the tools of knowledge. For example, if your audience has poor reading skills, a book is out of the question (e.g., a five-year-old child to whom you are trying to sell). If your readers don't have a CD-ROM player on their PCs, you may not want to put text onto that medium. If only a third of your employees use Lotus Notes, a company newspaper or monograph may be your best vehicle for getting to all of them.

Closely related to each of these questions is the level of detail and complexity of the issues you want to discuss, a topic we reviewed in the first two chapters of this book. If the topic is complex, you may need verbal communications, using video conferencing or a 50-page monograph. On the other hand, if you have a half-dozen quick points to make about your company's position and insights on an issue, a flyer might do the trick.

If an engineer needs to understand what all other engineers in the firm have learned *so far* about a particular problem with an automotive engine, a real-time database with white papers, an electronic chat room, and an electronic competency network would be perfect, not a book on automobile engines. Yet those same engineers, if seeking information about the theoretical operations of a combustion engine, would probably prefer to read about it in their spare time (say, while flying on a business trip) and in book form rather than to log on to a company intranet site for the same information. And, for a case history, they would probably enjoy an article on the engineering history of Ford Motor Company's development of the Mustang in the 1960s, complete with photos and blueprints.

Every company communicates knowledge either by design or accident. Even a company that publishes only calling cards is communicating through publications. If there is a central message in this book, it is that publications come in many forms and deliver an enormous variety of messages. The more lengthy or complex a publication, the greater the odds that knowledge is being communicated, not just data. Selecting which vehicle to use is crucial.

Now let's take a look at an example: your local telephone company. It publishes in paperback white and yellow pages of data that it knows it can get to every customer. There is no worrying about the customer having PCs or networks, and no requirement for deep insight into telephony. The same company also makes this information available by customer request to an operator to look up the data in a telephone database. In France, a phone user can do that on-line because everyone who has a telephone has a terminal for that purpose. That same firm publishes manuals that explain to repairmen how to fix thousands of different types of problems encountered daily by users of the phone system and by those who maintain the network. These employees also have access to databases of information and communicate among themselves in formal settings to share insights (e.g., at staff meetings). They also attend classes in which knowledge is shared verbally and through class handouts (e.g., overheads, white papers, monographs, cards, and books). Videos on specific issues are published and made available both on-line and in cassette form for employees to take home to view.

To reduce the labor content of its work, your local phone company has probably automated many things, such as directory assistance. It wants to have fewer employees because personnel cost more than equipment. But it must have employees; so, to work with fewer numbers of them, those who are on the payroll must be able to do more work of better quality than before. That requirement means the telephone company must train its people and create a working environment where employees want to learn more about telephone operations. They need tools for that. Publications are such tools. That is why telephone companies have such a strong heritage of publishing all kinds of knowledge artifacts and in every conceivable medium. And, it is cost effective because they always need to reach out to thousands of employees on a particular issue.

Another example of what can happen illustrates the role of publications. In the early 1990s, the IBM Consulting Group conducted a large survey on the activities of CIOs, the folks who run computer operations for enterprises. IBM learned a great deal about what these people did, the issues they worked with, and the problems they faced. Since CIOs constitute a major community of customers, IBM published the results of their findings in monographic form. IBMers gave speeches at conferences on the results, and the CEO of IBM established an annual CIO conference where these kinds of issues could be discussed among peers. A byproduct of these various publications and events was the creation of a formal consulting competency around Information Technology Strategy, a topic of great interest to CIOs. Over the years, this competency worked on thousands of projects with clients, created an intellectual capital system on its related issues, and from time to time published or spoke publicly on IT strategy. Meanwhile, thousands of IBM consultants acquired increasingly sophisticated skills in the subject, which they applied in client engagements and support of IBM's own internal use of computing. Today, one would be hard pressed to think IBM consultants could not develop IT strategies for just about any company or government agency. Publications started the process, led to the capture and sharing of information, then to knowledge, and, finally, to application in ways that made sense to customers and IBM's stockholders.

Why Cement Is So Important to a Bricklayer

 Ever watch bricklayers for an extended period of time? When they start in the morning, they stack a large pile of bricks at the spot where they will be working that day. Next, they carefully mix sand and cement with water, stirring it around, adding a little of one ingredient or another, stirring again. They hover over the container or pile of sand and cement, getting the mixture just right. By *just right* they mean of a consistency that will allow them to do three things. First, the mixture must contain the right combination of ingredients so that when it is dry, it will hold the bricks together for many decades, possibly centuries, in the face of local weather conditions and anticipated wear and tear on the bricks.

Second, the mixture must be pliable for as long as the bricklayer needs. This means it must not dry before he has had a chance to slap it on top of the brick and get it positioned in the wall being built. If it dries too soon, he has wasted cement, has to clean out the cement mixture, and has to start all over again. So, he has learned with experience and training how much to make, given his understanding of how long it has to sit before it is all used.

Third, the bricklayer wants a look to the cement that adds to the overall appearance of the structure he is putting up. Some cement has to be light colored; some, gray or brown. In short, like the bricks themselves and any other part of the wall or structure, cement, which is very visible, must contribute to the overall desired effect.

Also watch what bricklayers do with their tools. Trowels are washed before and after use so that cement and dirt does not cling to the tool or cause it to be ineffective. The cement mixer at the start of the day is often cleaner than our tools at home. The machine is washed before and after use so that it does not compromise the quality of the cement. Often, the physical site is also washed before cement is made. In short, the tools and environment are carefully prepared so that the bricklayer can exploit the tools and ingredients along with his skills to do the best job possible.

Our bricklayer is very much like an author or manager of a knowledge management effort. Like them, he worries about applying the right knowledge at the right time. He worries about the results achieved, based on experience and prior knowledge. If a new form of cement is invented, we can count on him learning about it and trying it on a project, particularly if the architect calls for its use. If tools are not collected and cleaned, the bricklayer runs the risk of not doing a good job. Along the way, he learns from experience how best to combine his knowledge, ingredients, supplies, and project objectives. The process is organized, the knowledge applied for tangible results. All aspects have to work together. All this is what makes our bricklayer a skilled worker in demand.

We need skilled workers in all jobs in an organization, from a well-trained, experienced CEO to a brand-new hire right out of college. Taking the time to develop these skills with the right tools and ingredients is what, at the end of the day, has to happen in a world in which knowledge is becoming the new gold of advanced economies.

SUMMARY

To a large extent, publishing and knowledge management in business environments tend to exist independently of each other. Some publishing always seems to be going on, especially in very large corporations. Much of this publishing is in support of specific activities (e.g., maintenance and training) or to describe products (e.g., car manual), but increasingly we are seeing business publications ranging from articles to complex videos, although usually in the form of articles and books. More than ever, these publishing activities are coordinated across the entire enterprise rather than simply allowed to pop up here and there at the whim of individuals or departments. The act of coordinating development of intellectual capital to publications makes good sense: published knowledge artifacts are well-tried channels for distributing information and capturing mind share. As companies implement knowledge management, they see publications both as a way to express their thoughts about a variety of issues and as a vehicle to improve the knowledge of employees. In other words, reading, not merely writing, is part of the process.

We touched only briefly on reading in Chapter 2 when we discussed how one became an expert. But now, we are seeing corporations expand what used to be almost an upper management practice—executives distributing to their direct reports a book or reprint of an article of particular relevance to the firm. A CEO may have sent copies of a book by Michael Porter to his staff in the early 1980s; a vice president, copies of a Steven Covey book to her department heads. Companies are now expanding the practice. For example, AT&T has a quarterly book club in which a book is selected and then made available to a wide audience within the firm. As individuals within a company publish, it is becoming common to see an executive distribute a copy to each employee associated with that part of the firm from which the publication came. Consulting firms routinely give each consultant and manager a copy of all books and articles published by a colleague. Those major consulting firms that are just beginning to understand knowledge management still do not follow this practice. However, leaders in consulting in the area of knowledge management do.

You will hear executives complain about the cost of sending reprints of articles or copies of books to employees. Let's look at the issue. A reprint of an article costs about one to two dollars. Books can be acquired for 30 to 45 percent of list price. In other words, books cost less than $20 each. Spark an idea in one employee out of a hundred, and the cost of one hundred copies of anything appears as pocket change. Get an entire organization to adopt the ideas in one book, and you have added a major positive component to your corporate culture. Send those people out for a one-day seminar, and the course fee is ten to twenty times or more than the book price, and the message will not even stick as well because it takes less effort to attend a seminar than to read a book. In other words, an executive cannot afford to deny employees major publications in their field of expertise.

Learning More About Publishing

This chapter points out where to learn more about how to get your intellectual capital published and distributed. This book could not cover everything nor list all sources of additional information, but this chapter will show you how to find out everything you need to know.

A FEW GREAT BOOKS TO READ

There are two general topics about which there is good published material to go to right away: writing and publishing; and intellectual capital.

Since most individuals are concerned about skills development and writing, let's deal with this one first. If you go into any bookstore in the world, you will quickly come to the conclusion that every publisher has published a book on how to publish. Almost all are competent in dealing with writing, grammar, style, and the tasks of finding publishers and agents. Just pick out a couple and you are in business. Now for several publications that are a must-have for your library.

- *A Manual of Style* (Chicago: University of Chicago Press, various editions). This is the Bible of the publishing world on how to produce a book. When you have any questions about style, content, how to create an index, design of a book, etc., this is where you find an answer. A related publication is the *Chicago Guide to Preparing Electronic Manuscripts for Authors and Publishers* (Chicago: University of Chicago Press, various editions). It does not really matter which editions of these books you have, the differences from one to another are not significant.

- *Simon & Schuster Handbook for Writers* by Lynn Quitman Troyka (Englewood Cliffs, N.J.: Prentice Hall, 1990 and subsequent editions). This is the grammar and style book you will love. This is the book to go to when you have questions about grammar, split infinitives, but also about how to organize your thoughts, get them down on paper, and clustered in evenly balanced sections and chapters.

- *Ulrich's International Periodicals Directory* (R.R. Bowker, published every year or two). This is a standard reference book that lists thousands of journals and magazines by subject and title, and gives their circulation and addresses. Don't buy it, just use it; every public library has a set.

- *Books in Print* (R.R. Bowker). This reference work is published in three versions: by publishers, by authors, and by book titles. This is the list all publishers use to register English language publications, primarily U.S. and British, currently in print. This is where you find out who has published on your topic. The volumes appear annually and are organized by author and subject. *Forthcoming Books in Print* is published quarterly in the same format as *Books in Print*; it lists what will be coming out over the next several months. Like the basic volumes, it gives full bibliographic citations and publication dates. Don't buy these; your public library and every book store has them.

♦ *Outsmarting the Competition: Practical Approaches to Finding and Using Competitive Information* by John J. McGonagle, Jr. and Carolyn M. Vella (Sourcebooks, Inc.). The authors originally published this book in 1990; it is still current and practical. Even if you have to hunt through secondhand bookstores, get it because it shows you how to gather data, turn it into useful information, and figure out how to apply it in business terms.

These are the only things you need. You don't even have to own a dictionary or a thesaurus if you write on a PC because your word processor has a spell check function. Please use it! You have no idea how many people don't!

Learning how to create and exploit intellectual capital is a different story. First, it is just now an emerging field of interest to business management, so the amount of really good material on the topic is still limited. The book that got things started recently for many executives was *Intelligent Enterprise* by James Brian Quinn (New York: Free Press, 1992), in which he explained how knowledge- and service-based systems were changing the nature of work and business. Since many believe that the ability of an organization to learn from its experiences is critical, learning how that is done becomes important. For your initial education, read a book on Japanese practices by Ikujiro Nonaka and Hirotaka Takeuchi, *The Knowledge-Creating Company* (New York: Oxford Univeristy Press, 1995). It reads well, is very tactical, and easy to find in bookstores. Since knowledge is also acquired in less formal ways, you will find it useful to read a fascinating book on how managers get the information they need: *The Information Mosaic* by Sharon M. McKinnon and William J. Bruns, Jr. (Boston: Harvard Business School Press, 1992). Finally, for an anthology of newly published material, you might want to look at *Knowledge Management Yearbook* by James W. Cortada and John A. Woods (Boston: Butterworth-Henimann, published annually); it always contains selections of material on learning and knowledge creation. The same publisher also produces a series of anthologies on various aspects of knowledge management, the only such series published anywhere.

While our yearbook will keep you up-to-date, there are other sources of insights on knowledge management. The best introduction to the subject is *Working Knowledge: How Organizations Manage What They Know* by Thomas Davenport and Laurence Prusak (Boston: Harvard Business School Press, 1997). The book defines knowledge management, what firms do to exploit knowledge, and how. It also includes specific examples and case studies. So far, this book is the only one available that covers the entire subject. It is short and easy to understand.

CLASSES AND SEMINARS TO TAKE

The two issues are: training for authors and help for those running corporatewide programs. Each is resolved differently.

For authors, the two questions to answer are "How do I write for publication?" and "How do I get published?" The first topic is best covered by creative writing classes taught by English departments at local community colleges and other institutions of higher learning. Journalism or English departments of colleges and universities often also teach semester-long classes on writing. Writing on technical topics is often also a course offered both by engineering and journalism departments. High-tech companies frequently hire consultants to teach one- to three-day seminars on technical writing as well. If you work for a large high-tech company, like Hewlett-Packard or IBM, you will find that from time to time, the internal training folks offer seminars on writing articles, books, and technical literature. If not, they know how to get that kind of training put together, so call them for help.

There is less help on how to get published. The first step would be to find someone in your company who can mentor you. Second, when writing is taught internally within a company, you usually also get a heavy dose of how to publish because the instructors are often consultants who teach the topic and publish themselves. You might also turn to the communications organization within your firm for advice on help, but also look to your local college or university journalism department. Some of the guides on publishing readily available at your local bookstore also list seminars and providers of training on the topic.

After all is said and done, getting a mentor is still the best way to find out how to publish. Taking a class on writing if you need it and then doing it is the best way to learn how to put thoughts down on paper.

Running a corporate publishing initiative is an entirely different matter. Here there are no convenient classes, let alone publications (other than the book you are reading now). Here the best sources are consultant firms that have the following consulting capabilities:

◆ Marketing programs

◆ Public relations

◆ Corporate change management

◆ Learning and knowledge creation

◆ Publishing connections and experience

With these firms, you are looking for both knowledge on how to run programs and skills on designing publishing, mentoring, and training processes. Some of this work is done by public relations firms; most has to be performed by management consulting firms. There are four ways to find out whom to call in for consideration.

◆ Look at *Consultants and Consulting Organizations Directory*, published by Gale Research Company, and periodically published with updated information. This is a directory of many consulting firms, their specialties, addresses, and so forth.

◆ Consult with other firms that have publishing programs or that have a reputation for well-managed intellectual capital, to find out who can help or with whom to benchmark.

◆ Consult with magazine and book publishers, especially those that publish a great deal of material from a company, e.g., editors of a mass-distributed publication published by a service firm, not a publisher.

♦ Consult the Internet and on-line bibliographic guides listing who is publishing on the subject.

All of these sources will eventually make you the source others come to. Finding experts to help is becoming easier since companies are launching intellectual capital management processes, creating in their wake a growing number of experienced experts and sources of help.

A major source of help on linking knowledge management and publishing is experts on knowledge management, such as consultants in the field. They also normally have experience in writing, so they can go beyond simply discussing knowledge management and take you quickly to the artifacts of knowledge management, of which publications is one.

ELECTRONIC SOURCES OF HELP

The biggest new source of information to emerge since the mid-1990s for information on all kinds of things is the Internet. The list of sources of information on the subject of publishing is growing rapidly, but here is a short list of sites to get you started:

Writers' Resources on the Web

`http://www.interlog.com/-ohi/www/writesource.html`
Covers all aspects of the writing and publishing craft with other hot sites to click on. This site is also being combined with another, so to bookmark, use

`http://www.inkspot.com/-ohi/inkspot/`

Virtual Library Publishers Writer's Resources

`http://www.comlab.ox.ac.uk/archive/publishers/other.html`

Provides pointers to other lists and information relevant to publishers, such as about various publishers, retailers, book catalogs and book clubs, to mention a few.

BookWire: The First Place to Look
`http://www.bookwire.com/`
A comprehensive source of information on book-writing. Has everything from lists of author tours to book reviews by topics, book awards; lists over 900 publishers, 500 booksellers, and over a thousand other resources.

Book Stacks-Books.com
`http://www.books.com/scripts/place.exe`
Also known as "Publisher's Place," lists publisher's on-line catalogs. This is a good place to electronically browse catalogs to get an idea of who publish books on your topic.

Publishers' Catalogues Home Page
`http://www.lights.com/publisher/us.html`
Like the previous citation, lists publishers of all types, with pointers to their on-line catalogs.

Publishers' Catalogues Home Page
`http://www.lights.com/publisher`
A Yahoo-accessed file, it is also a catalog of publishers, covering many countries, each with its own links.

Inkspot: Writers' Association
`http://www.inkspot.com/-ohi/inkspot/assoc.html`
Not only lists associations but also points to other sites listing yet other groups of writers. Identifies these organizations and their primary focus. Check this one out!

Manage Your Writing: Introduction
`http://wyn.com/komei/writing/manage00.htm`
For those people who want to write effectively on business topics. It has twelve chapters on the writing process, covering such issues as planning the work, how to write, improving one's writing, and making one's point.

Business Writing
`http://www.interlog.com/-ohi/www/biz.html`
> Another way of getting information on the subject, including sites on marketing, publishing, resumes, articles and essays, courses and workshops. Includes bibliographies, materials from university-level teaching classes, and free electronic newsletters. This is a good site to go to!

Every magazine and journal, it seems, has a page. The sites above can get you to many of these. The list of publishing-related pages could fill a book. Curiously, intellectual capital management is only just beginning to appear in a scattered manner on the Internet, so it is too early to compile a comprehensive list of these.

On the general theme of knowledge management, the number of Internet sites is expanding rapidly. For the most complete list currently available, see the 1999-2000 edition of the *Knowledge Management Yearbook*.

NETWORKING IN THE PUBLISHING WORLD

We have provided a series of suggestions throughout this book about networking with publishers. There is no need to repeat these messages. However, there are some additional thoughts that are appropriate to add.

The world of editors is an industry onto itself. There are competent members and others about whom you wonder. However, either you the individual or you the architect of a corporate publishing strategy should develop a strategy for getting inside this world and becoming comfortable with it. At various places in this book, I have suggested that you simply call an editor and establish a relationship, ask questions about your ideas, what is publishable, and so forth. If you are managing a corporate program, you will want to ask these people what is hot in the market and why, who is buying and reading materials, and who are the publisher's key competitors. Understanding trends in publishing of articles and books, videos and CDs is not only useful for placing material but is yet another source of market data that can be passed on to product designing, marketing and sales, consulting, and service providers. Publishers are an excellent source of market information rarely tapped by marketing and sales, let alone other functions in a company. So use them to validate other sources of data.

But beware of their bias. A publisher makes no money in just reporting through articles and books that things are the same. They are constantly looking for trendiness, ways to hype a topic, how to exaggerate a changing situation. For example, publishers love to bring out articles and books that declare there is a computer *revolution* underway, that everyone is climbing on the Internet, and that you should, too. The fact is, computer technology and its adoption is an *evolutionary* process, and as of this writing (1999), less than 20 percent of the U.S. public has used the Internet. But those facts don't sell as well as the hype. So, when talking to an editor about trends and what is hot, either pander to the hype or discount what you hear. Most editors do not conduct formal marketing studies to determine what potential book buyers want; instead, they rely on their personal experience and on what their colleagues in the same publishing house and elsewhere think are publishable topics. That is both good and bad. It is good in that if you can persuade an editor that the world needs your article or book, you are in. It is bad in that once editors make up their mind that a topic is soft or dead, you could have the greatest publication in the world and it might not get published. Thus, perception and timing become important variables in the equation. But, there is almost always an editor willing to publish your intellectual capital and to work with your company.

The publishing world is really a small one in that editors all know each other; they move around from publisher to publisher with a gypsylike migratory pattern. One can lead you to another, give you insight about other editors, or blackball you. The best authors and corporate program managers build alliances and add more contacts to their repertoire, doing these things on a continuous basis. As an author, I try to meet by phone with a new magazine, journal, or book editor every two or three weeks. Program managers in publishing should be on the phone several times a week trying to place material, identify projects, and just expand their insights and contacts. You don't even have to go to a publishing trade show to do that; however, those are wonderful opportunities to meet and deal with many publishers in several days. *Publishers Weekly* is the best source for worldwide information on these conferences. Almost all national annual conventions of professional associations (both academic and industry) will have editors and publishers present. Either turn up and stick out your hand and introduce yourself or set up prior appointments to meet at these events. Nothing like the personal touch!

All publishers are in constant need of new material. If you can bring authors, manuscripts, and ideas for publications to them, you wind up on their Rolodex file as someone with whom they want to stay in touch. Over time, they will invite you to write articles and books, participate in TV and radio programs, and film videos on your area of expertise. At the same time, you will be asked to critique articles and books being considered for publication. Academic journals and book publishers usually have two or three readers for every proposed project and manuscript. Some publishers will pay you an honorarium for this kind of work. This activity allows you to influence what gets published, by whom, and where, and makes it possible to network with authors who, in turn, have their own access to other publications. Reading this kind of material reinforces your confidence in your own expertise and can be a useful time burner, if you spend a lot of time on airplanes, for example! These editors in turn tell others of your expertise. How do you think reporters find people to quote in *The Wall Street Journal* or in *The New York Times*? They call their contacts, some of whom are editors and authors.

BUILDING INTERNAL KNOWLEDGE ON PUBLISHING

This subject is not about running publishing programs (the topic of Chapter 9). Rather, there is the requirement for organizations to create a culture in which knowledge about how to publish is accumulated and shared. Where this occurs, a number of conditions are evident.

First, you see a great deal of one-on-one mentoring of new authors by employees experienced in these matters with or without recognition or additional compensation. It's what experienced authors do. Authors are encouraged, novice writers seek them out, and management applauds and gets out of the way of this activity.

Second, people who publish are honored, are highly respected, and are sought out for advice on the subjects about which they write. Existing company awards and recognition events are perfect for this exposure. You do not have to hand out too many awards before publishing grows. Bonus for publications seems like a good approach, but in fact it is bad because it just encourages publishing quantity, and not necessarily quality.

Third, experiences of published writers are overtly shared. That could be done through the publishing initiative, but in many firms this sharing occurs when authors are invited to write about their experiences in company newsletters or to present their insights at internal gatherings.

All three activities are reflections of organizations that have a culture that values knowledge and its artifacts. There is a cerebral tone to their culture. You see that culture, for example, in high-tech companies, like Microsoft, IBM, or H-P. Where work is intellectually demanding, the opportunity for creating such a culture exists because of necessity. Publishing useful material is simply an extension of a preexisting environment. Tougher, is doing this in a culture that does not have the requirement for intellectual curiosity. At the risk of insulting some readers, I can't image a manufacturer of bricks or a trucking firm having such a culture. But don't be surprised, whoever thought the U.S. Army would have formal programs to reflect on its daily activities? We don't think of armies as encouraging honest intellectual analysis, regardless of rank.

The key is not just launching publishing programs; it is the application of knowledge management best practices among those who publish that expands institutional understanding of the topic. You begin with programs to jump-start the process, but then create opportunities for authors to share knowledge in exactly the same way you would share insights of engineers, sales people, and the financial fraternity within any firm. The subject of writing and publishing gets treated the same way as these other business knowledge competencies.

I would like to end this book with a story about my personal experience at IBM. In my early years I wrote articles and books, oblivious of the firm. My colleagues and managers essentially ignored my weekend hobby. In time, however, individuals sought me out, having read something of mine, to share their desire to publish. I advised them, and in time (by the end of the 1980s), the number coming to me reached over 50 a year. I taught one-day seminars on publishing from time to time within the firm regardless of what job I had. I found internal training centers that provided me channels for announcing the availability of a seminar and that sometimes even provided me with a classroom. Occasionally, I used a conference room. The word spread, and others asked, "When are you going to teach the class again?" Those seminars provided the meat of the book you are reading.

So it went for many years. By the early 1990s, one could find short seminars within the firm on how to write articles, others on technical writing (for the folks who write all those manuals that computer people use). Periodically some organization would write a monograph or paper, often published through IBM's internal publishing arm, the folks who bring you all those manuals. In time, I was asked to write an article for some company newsletter, on other occasions to run a workshop as part of some company function. Others began to do the same thing. Now, authors within the firm frequently talk to each other, compare notes, help novice writers, and provide access to editors for the new and experienced authors. In short, it has developed into an informal, silent fraternity. The result has been increased interest in publishing on topics relevant to the firm and more publications. By the end of the 1990s, more articles, monographs, and books were being published by IBMers in any one year than often had been published in whole decades. Yet the number of employees in the firm is smaller than a decade ago.

The process I just described developed simultaneously in North America, Brazil, and in Western Europe. By the mid-1990s, IBM employees on different continents were sharing publishing experiences across borders. I even collaborated with a Brazilian colleague to write a book on quality management practices. It was a wonderful experience.

The one great exception was the development laboratories and the IBM Thomas J. Watson Research Center. These organizations, like Bell Labs or a great research university, were always staffed with employees who did research, had a strong academic heritage, and needed to publish in order to accomplish their work. They were prolific, like their colleagues in academia. But the great change I noticed in IBM, beginning in the 1980s, was the growing interest in knowledge management and its link to publications in those parts of the business that I thought never published: sales, distribution, consulting, technical support, management. Today, we have general managers who publish articles and books. A quarter of a century ago that would have been unimaginable. Today, general managers encourage publications, even allocate resources to make that happen. Yet they are as tough-minded about the "bottom line" as a manager would be in any competitive industry. Why? For the reasons we have discussed throughout this book. In short, through their valuing of publications and knowledge, they have subconsciously created a corporate culture that reflects the kinds of behavior Brian Quinn and so many others said were necessary for companies to have if they were to compete on competencies, to operate as learning organizations.

The U.S. Army and Publishing: The Case for Historical Publications

Since we picked on the U.S. Army earlier in this chapter, yet applauded its implementation of knowledge management practices, it makes sense to look at that institution one more time. As part of its sense of identity, the Army looks to history for lessons to govern the behavior of today's soldier. Experience has proven the wisdom of this practice. In *A Guide to the Study and Use of Military History*, a 500-page guide for soldiers and officers alike, the readers are encouraged to study and publish. The book includes a detailed account of how the military

does this organizationally. One contributor to the volume (pages 393-394), Joseph R. Friedman, gives us an example of the values of the military.

> You who have read these words have been to the requisite military schools. You have had the courses in History and English considered necessary to attain your present state of grace. You may have had battlefield experience. Perhaps you wear a gold or silver bar. You might even sport twin bars or a gold oak leaf on your shoulder. Many of you have stars in your eyes. Having been exposed to appropriate education and training in how to study, and profit from, written military history, you have read the wise words purveyed in the preceding chapters of this book. Now you are presumably ready to advance your career to the point of producing fruits of your own that will nourish your colleagues and specialists in the broad acres of the field of military history.

Colonel John E. Jessup, Jr., commenting on history in the same manual (page 302), could easily have been talking about any business topic and the value of knowledge reflected in his army when he wrote:

> The basic Army regulation on military history and the annual programs provide for historical activities of departmental staff agencies and Army commands worldwide. Army staff agencies send unclassified material to the Center of Military History for the annual Department of the Army Historical Summary and compile classified annual historical reviews for their own use and for preparation of later histories. Major commands and some subordinate commands also prepare annual historical reviews and monographs on selected current topics. The Army encourages its leaders, commissioned and noncommissioned, to make full use of military history. Individual units preserve and use their own history to promote pride and self-esteem...
>
> The Army's historical program is comprehensive with organizational threads extending from the secretariat through the departmental staff and the Center of Military History to stateside and overseas commands, agencies, installations, and units. The program is designed to preserve and use the military record for the many purposes that history serves.

If an Army can do all of that, can a business enterprise ignore the possible benefits of promoting and publishing what it knows? The U.S. Army has much to teach management about getting the word out. Clusters of knowledge, like bricks, are the building blocks of an organization's competencies. This is as true for the private sector as it is for any government agency.

Source for quotes: John E. Jessup, Jr. and Robert W. Coakley, *A Guide to the Study and Use of Military History* (Washington, D.C.: Center of Military History, United States Army, U.S. Government Printing Office, 1979).

SUMMARY

A combination of strategies is needed to learn more. Books and copyeditors will show you how to write; writing itself is the best way to learn how. Reading publications in the subject areas you work in and write about remains the best way to learn about issues, topics for publications, and thought leaders. Networking with editors and publishers is the piece that brings it all together. If you had to build a value chain for yourself, subscribe to Michael Porter's concepts of strategic advantage, and be part of the trendy world of intellectual capital management, it all boils down to those three sets of tasks—writing, reading, networking. Be a pack rat: collect information, publications, and contacts. Over time you will have built for yourself, your friends, and your company a publishing ecology that provides everything you need: new intellectual capital, personal skills, outlets for your ideas and ego, a platform for your company, and all the support functions to ensure success. In summary, whether for an individual or a corporation, these environmental "must haves" include research, people writing, graphics and word processing, ghost writers, access to publishers, experience, and contacts. Distribution of your intellectual capital thus leads you to a collection of partnerships with mutual dependencies:

- You with an editor
- An editor with you or your company
- A publisher's marketing arm doing right by your articles and books
- You helping a publisher through self-promotion, distribution, and cooperation in being accessible to the public

The reason lions are kings of the jungle is because they figured out how to develop core skills, gain access to herds, watering holes, and members of the opposite sex, and all within a climate supportive of their primary objectives. They do it individually and in groups, just like people and companies. Should you do anything less?

Index

D

Deming, W. Edwards, model of an expert, 26
Deployment, to publish, 153-158
Drucker, Peter F.
    history of *Management*, 135
    paid his dues, 73
    role model for experts, 33

E

Editors
    as publishers, 71-72
    questions to authors, 97
    role of, 3-8
    working with, 69-70
Electronic publications
    described, 52-55
    precautions with, 75-77
Emerson, Ralph Waldo, poem by, 140
Employees, reasons they don't publish, 146-147
Expenses, for corporate publishing programs, 162-165
Expertise
    described, 21-39
    how to develop or expand, 27-37
    writing about what you know, 60-61
Experts
    characteristics of, 24-27
    communication departments and, 66
    how recognized, 22-23

F

Fahey, Liam, on knowledge management best practices, 176-177
First Amendment, authors and, 119
Franklin, Benjamin, quoted on value of a career, 26
Free Press, 45
Friedman, Joseph R., quoted on U.S. Army values, 200

G

Gates, Bill, publishing intent of, 10
Ghost writers, role of, 69-71

H

Hammer, Michael, 85
    makes videos, 52-53
    publishing by, 10
Harry Schwartz Bookstore, role of, 132
Harvard Business Review, 43, 133
    circulation of, 42
    likes academic involvement, 113
    publishing in, 74
Harvard Business School Press, 45
    publishing with, 74
    what it publishes, 3
Hemingway, Ernest, writing habits of, 78

Hewlett-Packard, publishing
training at, 190
Higher education, publishing in
business compared to, 12-15
Hobbes, John Oliver, quoted on
importance of career, 26

I

Iaccoca, Lee, publishing intent of,
10
IBM
author's experience in, 198
conferences with Clemson
University, 156-157
early knowledge management
practices (1920s) of, 173
evolution of publishing
competency within, 198
measures of thought leadership
at, 161
publishing by, 147
publishing training at, 190
IBM Consulting Group, research
and publishing on CIOs,
182-183
IBM Global Services, 48
IBM Thomas J. Watson Research
Center, publishing at, 199
Information Technology Strategy,
an IBM competency, 182-183
Infrastructure, interest in knowledge management, 179-180
Intellectual capital
case for sharing, 144-146
role of communications
departments publishing, 66
who owns, 102-105

Internet
publications on, 54-55,
75-77
publishable topics, 5
sources on publishing,
192-194
Intranets, publications and, 77

J

Jefferson, Thomas, 38
role model, 18
Jessup, John E., Jr., quoted on value
of knowledge, 200
Job, role of publishing in, 11-12
Joiner, Brian, how he sold books,
125
Journalists, publishing topics of, 15
Journals
picking to publish in, 72
role in building expertise, 29

K

Kaplan, Robert S.
makes videos, 52
thoughts of, 161-162
Knowledge
codification of facilitated by
publishing, 169-170
sharing in firms that
publish, 197
types of, 27-29
Knowledge management
defined, 170-173
linking to publishing, 178-183

Watson, Thomas J., Jr., number of
     his books sold, 11
White papers, described, 42-47
Work
     habits of authors, 93-95
     organizing to write, 66-71
Writers, work habits of, 93-95
Writing, as organized activity,
     66-71, 92-95

X

Xerox, publishing by, 147

Y

Yourdon, Edward,
          publishing experience of, 75